A Platform With
No Timetable

Huang Chun-Ming

A Platform With No Timetable

Translated from the Chinese by
Howard Goldblatt

BALESTIER PRESS
LONDON · SINGAPORE

Balestier Press
Centurion House, London TW18 4AX
1010 Dover Road #01-800, Singapore 139658
www.balestier.com

A Platform With No Timetable: Collected Stories
Copyright © Huang Chun-Ming, 1973—2005
English translation copyright ©Howard Goldblatt, 2021

Saiyonara/Zhaijian from *The Taste of Apples*, by Huang Chunming, translated by Howard Goldblatt, Copyright ©2001 Columbia University Press. Reprinted with permission of the publisher.

Other stories first published in English by Balestier Press in 2021

Sponsored by Ministry of Culture, Republic of China (Taiwan)

ISBN 978 1 911221 16 6

All rights reserved. No part of this publication may be reproduced, stored in a retrieval system or transmitted in any form or by any means, electronic, mechanical, without the prior written permission of the publisher of this book.

This book is a work of fiction. The literary perceptions and insights are based on experience, all names, characters, places, and incidents either are products of the author's imagination or are used fictitiously.

Contents

Saiyonara / Zhaijian 7

Bright Red Shrimps 67

Mr. Presently 93

Blind Ah-mu 105

Swatting Flies 119

The Ghost-Eater Is Here 134

A Story of Nine Fingers 155

The Last Phoenix 157

A Platform With No Timetable 193

Listen to Me, All You Deities 199

Variations on a Canary's Lament 229

Dragon-Eye Well 243

Sayonara / Zaijian[*]

THE HUMAN CONDITION

I can't help but feel pleased with myself when I reflect on how I handled two onerous affairs over the past couple of days. The first was taking seven Japanese men out whoring with some of my countrywomen; the other was erecting a false bridge between those seven Japanese and a Chinese youth—in other words, the perpetration of a gigantic hoax.

This is how it all came about. Late yesterday morning our general manager placed a long-distance call to Taipei from our branch office in Kaohsiung, telling me to be at the airport by 12:10 to meet a Mr. Baba and six other Japanese. He told me repeatedly and in no uncertain terms to treat them well, as they had close business ties with our company. They had decided to go directly from the airport to the hot springs in Chiao-hsi. Since Chiao-hsi was so far out of the way, I recommended the hot springs of Peitou as a better choice.

"Everyone knows Chiao-hsi is way out in the country, that the girls there aren't as pretty as those in Peitou, and that the tourist accommodations leave a lot to be desired. But you see, they're

---

[*] The title is the Japanese and Chinese for "good-bye." The four sections of the story are titled after popular Japanese films.

looking for something out of the ordinary. Baba and his bunch are a '*Sennin gin kurabu*,' a so-called 'Thousand Beheadings Club.' They've been to Taiwan five times already—this makes the sixth —and Baba said he wanted the hot springs of Chiao-hsi added to their itinerary."

"Why not ask Assistant Manager Ye to accompany them, sir? I've got work piling up."

"No, no! Chiao-hsi is your hometown, so I want you to take them."

"But ..."

"This is company business, and important business at that," the general manager said somberly. Then he began to laugh. It probably struck him as funny that he was turning pimping into "important company business." At least that's what I figured.

At first I assumed there was no way I could refuse, but when I heard him laugh I mustered up the courage to try to get out of the assignment, just as the time signal blared in my ear and the operator asked, "Do you want to continue your conversation?" The general manager and I answered almost simultaneously: I said yes, he said no. Unfortunately for me, it was his call, and he hung up. I distinctly heard the click but instinctively shouted "Hello! Hello!" several times before dejectedly replacing the receiver. Unless I decided to quit and go home, it looked hopeless.

In my wildest dreams I never imagined I'd be a pimp someday. But in fact, this turn of events was neither as lightly achieved nor as simple as it sounds, for at the time I was in the throes of a painful psychological struggle.

As I slammed the receiver down, Assistant Manager Ye and my office-mates all turned to look at me. Assistant Manager Ye already had an inkling of what had transpired, especially since

I'd mentioned his name during the conversation, and as soon as I hung up he said in a loud voice, "So the general manager wants you to take a group of Japanese to the hot springs at Chiao-hsi, huh?"

"He wants me to be a pimp!" I said angrily.

Except for two female co-workers who lowered their heads, all the others burst out laughing. I sensed from their looks that they'd thrown down a challenge. Most of the time they considered me to be the most principled and straitlaced person among them, and in my speech and actions that's what I wanted to convey. So it seemed to me that they were eagerly waiting to see how I'd handle this pimping business. I hadn't expected to be put into such an awkward position by people who revel in the misfortunes of others. Actually, it wasn't simply a matter of doing a little pimping; if that had been all there was to it, I could easily have laughed at myself then and there and let it go. I could surely have managed that without any damage to my principles. The problem was, not long ago, a newspaper article had spurred me into attacking the Japanese meekly to take a group of seven Japanese men out whoring with some of my countrywomen. I was acutely aware that my colleagues would prefer to see me throw up my hands and quit. They'd reward me with looks of respect and envy and even be so magnanimous as to honor me with a round of hearty praise. Naturally, some would only be going through the motions, pretending they were really intent on my staying.

I knew that if I went ahead stolidly and met those Japanese, my image would suffer in my co-workers' eyes, and my work at the office would be affected. But all this was nothing compared to my deep-seated inner struggle.

My position as someone who has a pretty good grasp of recent

Chinese history has led me to abhor the Japanese. I was told that my grandfather, whose stories I'd loved listening to, had had his leg smashed by the Japanese as a young man. Then there was my middle-school history teacher, an unforgettable man we all respected, who had tearfully related to us episodes from the 1937-1945 War of Resistance against Japan. He told us how the invaders had come to China with battle songs heralding their heavenly mission of rooting out the unrighteous, euphemistically giving this vicious and evil war of aggression the title of "holy war." Meanwhile they had swept across China butchering and brutalizing untold numbers of innocent civilians. This history teacher, who was himself from Nanking, showed us a foreign magazine with photographs of the "rape of Nanking." We saw decapitated Chinese, pregnant women whose bellies had been slit open, and, most unforgettably, lines of Chinese, including mothers clutching their children, walking hand in hand into huge pits to be buried alive. I recall that my body grew rigid and hard as stone when I saw those pictures. Tears flowed as we listened to him, and we hated ourselves for being too young to have participated in the war, searching out the "Jap devils" and avenging our countrymen.

Who could have predicted, with all the changes in the world situation and the transformation of society in the twenty years that followed, that the seeds our history teacher had planted in our hearts as part of his educational mission would reach the present stage of development? Though I felt an occasional embryonic stirring, no opportunity for the seeds to sprout ever presented itself; or perhaps this awareness of mine had long since been washed away by the tides of time. Still, there is no way that something so deeply rooted in my conscience could ever be completely eradicated.

Now, however, not only could I not be hostile to Japanese but also, on the general manager's orders, I was being forced to accompany them to the hot springs at Chiao-hsi and keep them well entertained. Granted, any Chinese would have felt the same sort of contradictions if given such an assignment, but my position as someone from the town of Chiao-hsi added another layer of ineffable difficulty. What was I going to say to hometown friends when they asked me why I'd come home? The general manager had emphasized that he wanted me to take them because I was from Chiao hsi.

Damn it, I'm going to quit!
Quit?

Since coming to Taipei ten years ago, I've changed jobs at least twenty times, doing whatever I pleased. Several times during that period I didn't even have money to pay the rent, and there were occasions when I had to pawn things to get money to take my sick baby to the doctor. The clouded expression that settled upon my wife's f ace during those fearful days hasn't completely left her. If I refused to take this assignment, where would I find another job? Then there are the chest pains that have been bothering me in recent nights. I can no longer cope with these things as easily as I could in the past. In all honesty, this job has given my small family its first chance for stability. And the clouded look on my wife's face, the picture of fear and foreboding, is gradually giving way to wrinkles of laughter with our child's nascent attempts to speak and some other new tricks. Even his chronic bran-chitis seems to have disappeared.

Damn it! I've got to stay on!
Stay?

Principles I've held on to tenaciously for many years and that have formed my unique personality and temperament—are they to be cast aside now? Then why have them in the first place? It wouldn't seem like the real me without them. I know that my close friends would be surprised if I did this thing, and after having grown accustomed to hearing their praises, what would I do once their vision of me lost its luster? I figure that the hardest com promise to strike would be with myself, for if I put aside my principles, what would I have left?

But on the other hand, if I take that stance, wouldn't I be placing my ego above everything else? Wouldn't that be the shortsighted way to look at things? Am I so great that I need sacrifice nothing, even for my family? Especially since my wife and child don't necessarily share my principles. For even though she's an adult who can understand her husband's beliefs and their worth, and can even support them regardless of the strain they impose upon her, what about our son—a child who understands nothing at all? When he's hungry he has the right to cry for milk. When he's sick he has the right to be given medical attention. He has the right to demand of the world that he be allowed to grow up and become independent. I know I could not bear to shortchange my own child, for who knows, he may someday accomplish something great, and if not him, maybe his children. And it might turn out that the key to his future rested solely on whether or not I did this thing.

When my thoughts reached this point, I suddenly discovered what a bastard I'd been in the past. The greater part of those so-called principles of mine could in fact be summed up as a game of esteeming myself by looking down on everything else and prizing only those things that elevated and satisfied my own ego.

"I guess I've got to do this pimping job after all," I said in answer to the stares of my officemates, who were eagerly anticipating a quick resolution. Although I said it jokingly, I'd actually come to the decision with grim seriousness. I knew what they were thinking and had to construct a ladder to let my self-respect descend carefully if it were to remain intact. "Don't laugh. I'm going to try my hand at being a pimp. Why not?" I didn't really care if they were listening or not, I had to finish this simple but important speech. "If I don't take those seven Japanese today, someone else will. One way or another, seven of our countrywomen are slated for the chopping block." At first they were speechless; then they exploded into laughter.

"Hey! Huang, what's wrong? What kind of talk is that? You're not dealing with some antiprostitution commission." This statement by Assistant Manager Ye was followed by more raucous laughter.

"Now wait a minute. Listen, will you?" I didn't have anything else to say, but I couldn't just drop the subject. "As far as I know, not one of those girls chose this line of work . They're victims of their environment—sacrificing themselves for their families. Since I'm going to be a pimp, I'll show them how to bleed those Japanese. You know that the price of women is a gauge of national development—the cheaper the women, the more backward the place. There are countries in South America, for example, where a girl earns only eight pesos for a day's work picking coffee beans, whereas a fourteen year-old can earn sixteen pesos by sleeping with a man, the exact price of a cup of coffee in one of the big hotels. Don't laugh, that's the truth. In the eyes of the Japanese we're a backward nation. Even though we've made great strides, they hold us in contempt. Damn it, when I see them coming to Taiwan with all their airs of superiority, it makes my blood boil!"

"So you're going to help them get their kicks at Chiao-hsi?" This bold comment by the shy Miss Chen, who was obviously moved by what I said, came as a complete surprise. And it sparked another outburst of laughter; I laughed with them, though in fact I was troubled by the comment. After my efforts to build a ladder in order to gently lower my self-respect, the bottom had been kicked out from under me.

I couldn't let her comment pass, but what was I to say? My reaction of "Uh huh, uh huh" must have seemed pretty comical, since they all laughed.

Just as I was finding myself falling into a state of total embarrassment, I had an inspiration. I asked her, "If the general manager had given you this assignment, would you have taken it?" My heart let out a secret cry of alarm. If she said no, then what?

But before I had time to give it any more thought, she replied, "I'm a girl, so the general manager wouldn't ask me to."

During the laughter that ensued I shifted the object of my attack. "Assistant Manager Ye, would you have done it if the general manager had asked you to?" He stammered something as he laughed, and I continued, "During our phone conversation just a moment ago he said this was company business, important business!"

With an embarrassed laugh, Assistant Manager Ye said, "No question about it. Who'd dare refuse?" As I stood looking at them, smiles frozen on their faces, I was aware of how crafty a person I'd become.

THE SEVEN SAMURAI

By mid-day I was standing at the airport exit holding up a large piece of white paper on which I'd written WELCOME MR.BABA in big letters. I waved it feebly and with considerable embarrassment in front of arriving passengers. Before long a Japanese came up, looked at the sign in my hand, gave me a smile, then turned around and shouted in Japanese, "He's come, he's here. He's over here!" Out came four more, all of whom gathered around the first man, then turned to look back inside. They were jabbering back and forth:

"What about Baba *kun* and Takeuchi *kun*?"* asked the first man out.

"They're still in customs."

"I wonder why they're giving us so much trouble this time."

"It looks like they're only nit-picking with us Japanese."

"They're real bastards!"

"They even checked inside my pants." "Me too!"

"Really? Ha ha ... they didn't check mine."

"Come on now, they checked all four of ours!"

"Did they really examine your crotches?"

"Mm-hm. They made us take down our pants too. What's so embarrassing about that? Why not admit it?"

"Heh, heh ... now, if it had been young Taiwanese girls doing the examining, I'm sure we'd have been happy to oblige."

They laughed delightedly, laughter that appeared to wash away the anger caused by the inspection.

They were standing across from me, separated by a railing and

---

* The Japanese word *kun*, like the word *san*, means "Mister," though the former is much less formal and is used by friends.

five or six steps. I figured we'd made contact, so I might as well fold up the paper and put it in my back pocket—I could still see myself standing there a moment ago waving it in the air. "I made a goddamned fool of myself!"

The one who'd come out first thought I was talking to him. "Baba *kun* hasn't come out yet," he said. "Wait a moment, please." Once again they seemed anxious. "Do you think Baba ran into trouble?"

"How could he? He wasn't bringing any contraband in."

"Maybe on account of those nylon stockings and pantyhose?"

"No, of course not! We've brought them with us before without any trouble."

"Maybe so, but we brought in eighty pairs this time!"

"Those things are dirt cheap. If they want them, they can have the whole lot as a gift."

"This is such a letdown."

"Those sons of bitches!"

" … "

" … "

" … "

Since we were separated by some distance, I couldn't make out all their grumbling and wasn't sure what they were talking about.

The other passengers from their flight had all debarked and were on their way, and these men were still waiting for Baba and Takeuchi. One of them started toward me to say something, but a couple of the others called out at the same time, "They're coming out!"

Two short, stocky Japanese, their faces set tightly, emerged.

"Any problems?" asked their friends.

"What kind of problems could there be? They were just trying to make things tough for us. Damn, that makes me mad!"

"Oh, Baba *kun*, he's here," the man said, pointing to me.

A smile quickly appeared on Saba's face, and he led the others over to where I was standing. We exchanged business cards across the railing.

"Mr.Xu is in Kaohsiung … " I stammered.

"Never mind, we're aware that your general manager is henpecked."

"No, honestly, he couldn't make it back from Kaohsiung this time."

"What difference would it make if he could, since he's so henpecked?" Baba asked with a chuckle. "But the trip won't be wasted as long as we have Huang *kun* to accompany us."

"No …" I didn't know how to respond to him. Although not intended to, Saba's words had reminded me of my role as a pimp. Troubled as I was, I managed to say, "Well, I'll do my best, and I hope I don't disappoint you."

"Just looking at you, so young and handsome, we know you won't."

Damn, that sounded terrible! I wondered what they were thinking. "Baba *kun*, what are we waiting for?" they pressed him.

"Nothing at all!"

"Well, let's go then."

"Okay, let's go!" Then Baba said to me, "Huang *kun*, the success of this trip depends on you."

Their luggage was very simple: each had a bag slung over his shoulder, a parcel containing two bottles of imported liquor in one hand, and another small bag in the other hand. Since there were eight of us in all, we hired two taxis and headed directly from Taipei Airport for Chiao-hsi.

Although we'd exchanged business cards at the airport, I still wasn't sure who was Ochiai, who was Tanaka, and who was Ueno.

The only ones I knew were the last two to come out—Baba and Takeuchi—and Sasaki, whose name I learned later. I remembered him because he had a particularly long face, and because he'd been the first one out of the airport, the one who'd nodded to me. I was in the first taxi with Baba and two others whose names I didn't yet know, while Takeuchi, Sasaki, and the rest followed in the second car.

"Huang *kun*, how far is it to Chiao-hsi?" Baba asked.

"Well, if we don't run into any rain or fog on the mountain roads, two and a half hours should do it," I said. "That's pretty far!" said one of the others—the bald-headed one.

"How's that?" the man sitting between Baba and the other blurted out with a laugh. "It looks like Ochiai *kun* is getting impatient!"

"Bullshit! You're the one who's getting impatient!" But he was laughing.

"If you want to know the truth, Tanaka *kun* is getting impatient too." Baba joined the others laughing.

I turned in my seat in front and said, "No, I'm afraid Baba *kun* isn't telling the *whole* truth. He ought to have said *everyone* is getting impatient." They laughed and shouted their approval.

"I was right, wasn't I? This trip won't be wasted as long as we have Huang *kun* with us," Baba said. "He knows what's on our minds."

Damn him! God damn him ... I cursed to myself, though my face was all smiles. I was conscious of the fact that in ten years of working in the business world I had acquired the habit of masking my true feelings, which I'd always despised in others. Nonetheless, this sort of societal influence on an individual's habits was no different than the instincts of camouflage, protectiveness, alertness, and imitation that animals have developed in order to survive.

From our light banter of a moment before I learned that the bald-headed man was Ochiai and that the other one was Tanaka. As the taxi passed around the statue on Tunhua North Road and onto Nanking East Road, Tanaka looked behind him and said, "Tell him to slow down. The other taxi can't keep up." The others turned around to look.

"He's caught up—he's right behind us now."

"Don't worry," I said. "Both drivers know the way." They turned back around and quieted down for a moment. Baba blew out a puff of smoke.

"What's going on with the Taipei customs people lately?" he asked, looking exasperated. "They're coming down pretty hard on us Japanese."

"Yeah, I wonder why!" said Ochiai.

"It's a case of Tel Aviv guerrilla-phobia," I said reproachfully.

"Tel-a-what? What phobia is that?" asked Ochiai as he leaned over.

I could see that neither Baba nor Tanaka had understood either, so I said, "Last month at Israel's Tel Aviv Airport, wasn't it four of your countrymen who … ?"

"Oh, that! We know," Tanaka said in a subdued voice, while the others leaned back in their seats and nodded.

"That damned bunch of animals murdered all those innocent people in mere minutes." Then I added, controlling my anger, "So who can blame the customs people here?"

"Oh, of course," Baba said, "of course. But still it seems they're more sensitive here in Taipei … " Baba, Ochiai, and Tanaka tried to conceal their distress , but I could see it in their f aces.

"If they're so sensitive in Taipei, why didn't they just refuse to let you off the plane?" I paused. "Tel Aviv guerrilla-phobia is a worldwide phenomenon these days."

"Um, you've got a point there," Baba said softly.

"The Japanese youth of today are absolutely lawless." The look on Ochiai's face showed that he was trying his utmost to absolve himself of any blame. "Day in and day out they're shouting their opposition to one thing or another. All Japan is in a state of anarchy. As I see it, if things continue this way, the end result is going to be chaos."

As Ochiai finished, I felt an urge to settle some old accounts by reminding him that the previous generation of Japanese wasn't much loftier than the youth of today. The blood and stench of their aggression in China had left an indelible stain on the annals of history. But after seeing the unhappiness on their faces and a complete absence of the looks of superiority that Japanese people usually bring to Taiwan, my thoughts went unspoken and I let the matter drop. Instead I smiled and asked, "Why so glum?" I paused. "Did they confiscate anything of yours?"

"As a matter of fact, they didn't."

"We certainly didn't bring any contraband in with us."

"Then everything's fine. I was afraid they'd confiscated your swords," I said in jest.

"What swords?" Baba cried out nervously. The others stared tensely at me without making a sound.

"Huang *kun*, don't make jokes," said Ochiai. "What swords are you talking about?"

Seeing how edgy they'd become, I laughed even harder. "What swords do you think?" I asked. "The swords you use in your 'Thousand Beheadings Club,' of course."

They exploded into laughter as they caught the joke.

"Ha ha ... that's right, our 'thousand beheadings' swords! Ha ha ... "

"We couldn't hijack an airplane with those, could we? Naturally they wouldn't confiscate them! Ha ha ... "

Baba felt himself ostentatiously down below. "I'd better make sure," he said. "Maybe mine was confiscated without my knowledge."

To be honest, no matter how mischievous I was feeling or how much I wanted to get under their skin, this struck me as pretty funny.

Then Baba assumed the pose of a stage comedian and shouted in the loud and peculiar voice of a Japanese samurai:

The Way of the sword is the Way of man;
With the sword there is man;
As the sword perishes, so perishes man.

Ochiai and Tanaka were sitting beside him laughing. Ochiai informed me that Baba was incanting the final lines of their "Thousand Beheadings Club" manifesto. They were a happy bunch now.

"How many years have you had this 'Thousand Beheadings Club'?"

"Eight years. We seven are the only members," Baba answered.

"Why only seven?"

"Well, we were schoolmates in elementary and middle school, then we were together in the army, now we're business associates. How about that? Not something you see very often, is it? A lot of people want to join, but we won't let them."

"We may not have a large membership, but in Japan we're famous," added Ochiai with great pride.

"What's the special significance of the so-called thousand beheadings?" I asked.

Baba squinted conspiratorially and said, "In former days all samurai had but one wish, and that was to kill a thousand men during their lifetime."

"I don't imagine any of them ever made it, did they?"

"No, but it was the samurai's ideal, and anyone who didn't subscribe to it was not a good warrior. So in order to kill his thousand men, he had to constantly practice his art."

"What about your 'thousand beheadings'?" I pretty much knew already but asked just in case there was more to it.

"Heh, heh." Baba laughed cunningly. "The days of the Samurai Code are gone forever, and we can never again wander the earth wearing swords, killing and being killed. Besides, we wouldn't be samurai even if we could. What we mean by our 'thousand beheadings' is that we hope during our lifetime to sleep with a thousand different women. Heh, heh, do you follow me?" Baba looked smugly at the other members.

I was struck by how loathsome they were , but a smile must still have shown on my f ace, or they wouldn't have been so openly licentious. The terrible thing about it was, I didn't have to feign the expression.

"Have any of you reached your goal?"

"Not yet!" Ochiai blurted out. "A thousand may not sound like many, but in fact it's hard as hell …"

"A thousand is our ideal, so every time we get the chance, we travel: South America, Southeast Asia, Korea, Taiwan … these are places we visit often."

"You must spend a lot of money!"

"We weren't born with any, and we can't take it with us. As

long as you look at it that way, it's not so bad. Life is short, and you have to take your pleasures when and where you can. Isn't that right? That's something else all seven of us agree on." I never imagined that such a concept could be supported by a tragic-heroic philosophical foundation. Baba had given this explanation in complete seriousness.

"And that's not all. We have a principle that except for our wives, we can never sleep with the same woman twice," added Ochiai.

"Does it count as a breach of the club's rules?"

"No, but you see, there's a limit to every man's vitality. Doing it a thousand times is no mean task, so in order to achieve our club's objective, self-restraint comes naturally."

Even Tanaka, who had been sitting quietly in the corner of the seat, leaning back with his arms folded and a smile on his face as he listened to the others, added a comment. "Huang *kun*, there used to be a basement coffee shop in the downtown area by the name of …" He thought for a moment. "I can't remember the name. Let's see, did it have a barbershop upstairs … yes, it was a barbershop. Do you know if that coffee shop is still there?"

"Hm, a basement coffee shop …" I pondered for a moment. *The Barbarian doesn't have a barbershop upstairs, nor does the Literary Salon; then there's …*

They sat there talking as I pondered. Baba looked over at Tanaka and asked excitedly, "You mean the place where Akiko worked?"

"Right! Akiko's place." Tanaka too was growing interested.

"Huang *kun*, listen to me and you'll know right away what place he means," said Baba as he tapped me on the shoulder. "There's a very narrow door next to the barbershop," he said, using his hands to help describe it, "that's easy to miss if you aren't looking for it. That door is the entrance to the coffee shop. Now do you know where I mean?"

I shook my head. "No, I can't place it."

"That's strange!" Baba replied. "It's a famous place, very well known in Japan! How could you not know it?"

"I'm sorry, I just don't. What makes the place so famous?"

"Heh, heh, heh. There are girls there from all over, and they can do absolutely everything. Now are you sure you don't know?"

"No." I really didn't. Baba and Tanaka eyed me with knowing looks.

In his role as the upholder of fairness, Ochiai said, "I believe Huang *kun* when he says he doesn't know. In matters like this, tourists are better informed than local residents. Those places cater to tourists, not locals, so it's not so strange after all."

By rights I should have been grateful to him for getting me off the hook and saving me from embarrassment, but it seemed to me he'd attached entirely too much importance to the whole affair. What was the great loss of honor in not knowing about such a place? In fact, in Chinese society, this knowledge was in itself a loss of honor. I wondered how Japanese looked at such things and experienced a mild, passing anger.

"Ochiai *kun*," I said, "there's no need to make explanations for me. If you were to ask me something like where the Palace Museum is, or the History Museum, and I couldn't tell you, then I might be embarrassed. But in matters like this, well … ha ha ha …" I laughed then because I sensed that I was being too grim and that my words were making them tense. They nodded repeatedly, expressing agreement with what I was saying.

"Huang *kun*, you're right, of course. We didn't mean any harm."

"That's right, we didn't mean any harm."

I was quite adept at pretending. I laughed loudly, as if it were all a joke, and gradually they were affected by it. I was even able to squeeze out a few tears of laughter, and as I wiped my eyes I said, "So? Now who's being serious, you or me? I'll tell you the truth," I said with a smile, "I do know that basement coffee shop you're talking about. It's not there anymore. The police closed it down a while ago."

There was nothing the three of them could do but look at me and smile. Ochiai seemed about to say something, but just as he started to speak, something told him to let it pass. He sat up straight, then fell back against the seat.

"Huang *kun*," Baba said, "you're really something!" Afraid that this would lead to another misunderstanding, he added, "What I mean is, I really admire you."

"No, no ... ."

They began talking among themselves.

"I was right, wasn't I?"

"That's for sure."

"Oh, come now," I said.

Tanaka still sat there in his corner, smiling and nodding his head.

I was generally pleased with things so far, having gotten in at least a couple of licks.

"There are three of you ganging up on me," I said jokingly. "That's not fair." I looked at my watch. "We still have more than an hour before we get there, so if you can sleep, you ought to try—you need to conserve your energy."

"No, I'd rather chat with you. But maybe you feel like sleeping," Baba said. "No, I'd just as soon chat too."

"Huang *kun*, if we say anything out of line, don't let it get under your skin," said Ochiai with a grin.

"I won't, and the same holds true for you."

As the taxi passed through the mountain area known as Sea of Clouds, the driver put a cassette in the tape deck, a Chinese rendition of a popular Japanese tune.

Maybe due to the effects of the music, Tanaka looked out at the mountain scenery and exclaimed, "Would you look at that! This place looks just exactly like Aomori Prefecture!"

"I was thinking the same thing myself," said Ochiai a little incredulously. He lowered his head to look out the window. "Except there aren't any roadside apple orchards."

"Those grass huts look the same too. See, right over there." Baba pointed to some huts we'd just passed. "Even the song the driver's put on is authentic," I said.

"That, and your fluent Japanese," added Baba with a smile.

Damn it, that does it! I cursed to myself out of anger and a sense of injustice. If Saba's comment had been a calculated one, then I'd lost this round. I secretly observed his expression to see if he'd had any intention of wounding me. If he had, then I'd have responded with some verbal jabs of my own. But my observation told me he had no such intentions, even though I still felt uncomfortable. I couldn't help thinking that in their subconscious they still considered Taiwan one of their colonies.* No, not only in their subconscious; in reality, Japanese who come to do business in Taiwan, with their haughty, disdainful attitude, strut around as if Taiwan were their economic colony. I turned back around and looked at the mountain road ahead. Throughout the trip I'd been troubled by feelings of loathing. Baba and the others behind me talked and laughed as before, and although it seemed they

---

* Taiwan was occupied by Japan from 1895 till 1945.

were talking about me, I didn't pay any attention to them. I sat there with anger boiling inside me and a meek expression on my face; even if they were telling wondrous stories, it sounded very unpleasant to me.

Damn it! A pimp! I'll quit!

Quit?

I should have put my foot down the moment I finished my conversation with the general manager in the morning. But how could I just up and quit?

The psychological struggles that had raged in me after the morning phone call were upon me once more. Unable to bear the pressure of these contradictions, I rolled the window down, stuck my head out, and let the wind beat against my face. After taking a few deep breaths, I felt a little more comfortable. The taxi was just then passing above a mountain valley. I began taking in the scenery: I could see the floor of the valley below and a long, narrow mountain stream flowing through it. The strange thing was, the sight of this watery thread far down on the valley floor brought vague thoughts of history to my mind. Historical something? Something historical? I didn't know. I felt as if the stream were flowing through my heart, bringing with it feelings of depression and sadness.

Baba patted me on the shoulder and said, after I pulled my head back in the window, "Huang kun, would you please ask the driver to stop. We have to relieve ourselves." As our taxi pulled to a stop, the car behind us with Sasaki and the others also drove up. Giggling and laughing, they all got out of the cars, formed a line at the side of the road, and began relieving themselves. I stayed in the car, watching them, and as I noticed two tour buses approaching I began to be a little anxious for them. But just as the tour buses, which were full of passengers of both sexes, passed by, the men not only continued to leisurely joke and talk, some of them even turned around as they were taking a leak and smiled at the passengers. Years before, whenever people of the older generation spoke of the Japanese, they talked about how the men loved to piss by the side of a road. At the time I hadn't thought it was such a big deal, but seeing the men standing there in a row, oblivious to everything but taking a leak, I finally understood why the older generation had been so preoccupied with this idiosyncrasy, and why the Chinese called the Japanese "dogs" or "the four-legged ones."

After the tour buses had passed, the men were laughing loudly, and I could even hear Baba shouting out in that strange voice:

The Way of the sword is the Way of man;
With the sword there is man;
As the sword perishes, so perishes man.

YOJIMBO

It was three-thirty in the afternoon when we arrived at the Evergreen Hot Springs Lodge in Chiao-hsi. After they'd picked out their rooms, the seven of them debated for a while whether to eat first or to take a bath. Ultimately they agreed to have food and wine delivered to Saba's room.

Two middle-aged women in uniforms and wooden clogs quickly and efficiently brought a large round table into the room, after which they moved in the right number of stools. When they came in again carrying the dishes and chopsticks, they brought along three seventeen- or eighteen-year-old girls.

"These three are on duty," the waitress, whose name was Ah-xiu, said to me. The girls stood timidly off to the side. Ah-xi u pointed to the nearest one. "Her name is Xiaowen, the one next to her is Ah-yu, and the last one there is called Yingying." As their names were called out, the girls nodded for lack of anything better to do, then crowded together and began to giggle.

I gave a cursory introduction all around. The seven men looked the girls over from head to toe, causing them no little embarrassment. Xiaowen lowered her head and seemed to be looking at her own unattractive feet, with their short, stubby toes and painted nails, trying her hardest to draw them back in. My experience told me that these girls were fresh from the countryside; deep suntans acquired f rom years of working out in the sun hadn't faded much. I also had an occasional glimpse of dark scars left by insect bites and sores all over their calves. Though they were professional girls now, their timid expressions produced an effect of freshness in the eyes of those seven Japanese battlefield heroes. I could hear their muted discussion:

"Not too bad."

"Sort of earthy," said Baba, "but that might be just what we're looking for."

"They're all pretty young."

"They look to be about sixteen or seventeen."

Sasaki said something-what, I'm not sure-that made the others laugh, and laugh hard. The three girls stayed huddled together and even looked a little frightened, though for some reason they couldn't keep from laughing along with the men. The one called Xiaowen even turned and pinched Ah-yu and Yingying on the legs, causing them to scream out. Puzzled and startled, the

Japanese asked me what was going on.

"You three dimwits," Ah-xiu yelled to the girls as she set the table, "why aren't you over here helping me? I'll give you hell if you don't watch out!"

"Xiaowen here pinched us for no reason at all!" complained Yingying as she reached over between Xiaowen's legs. "I'll get even with you!"

"Help! Don't!" Xiaowen screamed and ran toward us.

"Madam! Look! Look here at your Xiaowen!" Ah-xiu yelled at the top of her lungs.

The waitress who'd come in with Ah-xiu joined the conversation, saying earnestly, "If you're not going to help, then at least sit down and behave yourselves. What do you think you're doing? These men here are Japanese guests, you know!"

The girls calmed down.

"They're still children," Baba said with a smile.

"Look here," Ochiai said as he embraced Xiaowen, who had gone over to him. "She's got quite a body. I want her." He lowered his head and looked at her cradled in his arms. "I like you. Do you understand?"

Xiaowen nestled softly in Ochiai's arms and asked me what he was saying. I told her. Suddenly she raised her head and pointed up at him. "Sex fiend!"

"Xiaowen! Watch your mouth!" Ah-xiu warned. Ochiai's curiosity was piqued. "What?" he asked. "I was just teasing him," Xiaowen said.

Ochiai asked again.

"She said you're a sex fiend," I told him.

He and the others laughed when they heard this. "That's right, I am." Then he gleefully pointed to the others. "And so is he, and so is he, and so is he ... all seven of us are sex fiends."

Sasaki, who was standing next to Ochiai, nonchalantly reached over to feel Xiaowen up, but she pushed his hand away.

"What makes you think you can do that?" she said. Then she struck the pose of a comic character in a Taiwanese opera and said with a smile, " 'A man takes no advantage of a good friend's wife.' Don't you know that?"

"Oh, you're a mean one, you are!" Sasaki said with a laugh in response to her actions.

"Huang *kun*, what's this child been saying?" Ochiai asked.

When I told him what she'd said, he was, of course, delighted, and proceeded to hug her even more tightly. "She really is a good girl!"

Sasaki, amused by all of this, reached out again and touched Xiaowen on the thigh. She promptly hit his hand, and they went back and forth like that while the others looked on with amusement.

"Sex fiend!" Xiaowen shouted. She wanted Ochiai to come to her defense, but he was trying to get her to hit Sasaki.

Naturally, Xiaowen hadn't meant anything in particular when she said "A man takes no advantage of a good friend's wife," but she wouldn't let any of the others except Ochiai touch her. I thought, *Xiaowen is, after all, Chinese, and though she may be a prostitute, in a contest to see who was more civilized—her or the Japanese—they'd lose. Maybe that's why we Chinese deride the Japanese by calling them "dogs."*

Before too long, Yingying and Ah-yu were also in someone's arms. It was then that the situation arose that caused me more discomfort and embarrassment than any other in my whole life. I was expected to translate all their meaningless small talk, and not just for one but for all of them. As I was not personally involved in a sexual liaison, most of what they were saying grated on my ears. Nonetheless, I had to translate all their comments for them. We have a saying in my hometown that goes: "The pig-stud farmer earns his pleasure." It means that someone who raises a boar to service others' pigs doesn't earn much, but at least he can get some vicarious thrills. In a rural society this kind of occupation is not looked upon as respectable and is usually reserved for old men who live alone. Although they don't have wives or children to keep them company, while the pigs are mating they remain alongside them, assisting in the process, using their hands to keep everything running smoothly, which is the source of some vicarious pleasure. Well, that's where this local saying comes from. Now that doesn't mean I'm using rural standards to look down on pig-stud farmers, for they at least get pleasure from their work. What was I going to get from mine?

Damn it! The more I thought, the angrier I got. But then, how could I lay all the blame at their feet? They weren't forcing me to do this. On the contrary, they'd treated me with politeness and courtesy. Their constant "Huang *kun* this, Huang *kun* that" was more or less designed to get on my good side. Then just what was it that made me feel Ihad to do it? Normally my understanding of society's influence on the individual is more theoretical than practical, but this time my comprehension came from personal involvement. Just as I was squaring off with the Gargantuan society, unhappily it sneezed, blowing me away to the very heavens as if I were caught up in a violent windstorm. Naturally, before me was not society in its entirety, only that portion under the control of Japanese economics. I think that must be why the Japanese come here with such feelings of superiority.

"Huang *kun*, have them send in a few more girls," Takeuchi said.

"Have them all come in. Tell them we have presents," said Baba as he turned and picked up a bag. "Look, we have all these presents." I told Ah-xiu to send them in, and she said they'd be coming right away, just as soon as the meal was served.

As promised, as soon as the first course arrived, twenty or so girls came to the room-some stood inside and some remained just beyond the door. Ah-xiu played the director, calling out, "You girls inside the room, step in closer. You girls outside, come on in." Then she said to me, "The three duty girls are already agreed upon. In addition to them, why don't you all choose one more apiece. You might as well have a few more." As she finished, she noticed there were still some girls who hadn't come into the room, so she yelled, "I told you to come in, but you just stand there! Well, don't accuse me of playing favorites when it's too late!"

Although several moved inside the room, at least seven or eight remained outside. The girls' faces were generally expressionless, but I could still tell who among them had been successful in their occupation and who had not. The ones inside the room manifested more confidence and pride than those outside. As I went out to ask the others to come into the room, I spotted one leaning up against the wall, her head lowered as she toyed disinterestedly with her fingernails. When she saw me coming out of the room, she looked up, then dropped her head even lower than before and turned her face to avoid looking at me. In that brief moment I had a good look at her face—one side of it was covered with an aboriginal tattoo. I vacillated for a moment. If I asked her to come in, her inferiority feelings would be even stronger than they were now, but if I didn't ask her, she'd be thinking, "The customer doesn't like my face," and would feel even worse. What to do?

In the midst of my indecision, not knowing how best to handle the situation, I took her hand gently and said, "I want you. Now won't you come in?" I saw the expression on her f ace-she was both startled and pleased—and in that instant her mind seemed to be cleared of many of its contradictions. Taking courage f rom this, I spread open my arms and affectionately herded all seven or eight of the girls into the room. My attitude toward them seemed to erase the feelings of inferiority they usually carried with them.

Baba was standing on a chair and weaving back and forth, causing everyone to laugh lightheartedly. He unzipped the bag draped around his neck and pulled out several pairs of nylon stockings, which he held up over his head as he shouted, "Is everybody in? Come on over! There's a pair here for everyone."

I urged the girls to go up and take them, but I never figured that as they surged forward, the six Japanese sitting on the floor would jo in the fray. Twelve hands reached out to begin feeling the girls up, resulting in a great deal of laughter and shouting. The men could not have been busier or hap pier, saying to themselves proudly as they probed:

"Aha! I felt it."

"Hey! Don't run away, those are nice titties."

"..."

I went up and grabbed several pairs to pass out to the few girls who wanted some but didn't have the nerve to go up and get them. They were all so delighted to get their hands on these things that even the ones who were molested during the handout felt it was worth it. Actually, stockings like those weren't that different from the ones sold in little stalls near the supermarkets in Taipei for about twelve dollars a pair-the packaging was a little nicer, and that's about all. Whatever this exchange between the Japanese and the girls constituted—whether it was to be a part of the whole deal or just a welcome gift—I couldn't help being reminded of their countrymen's posture in so-called Sino-Japanese economic and technical cooperation. *Damn it*—as these thoughts crossed my mind, I began feeling uneasy about myself again.

It was during all this grabbing and feeling that each of them selected the girl of his choice and began embracing her. Baba had his eye on one for himself, so he jumped down and threw his arms around her. The girls who remained, knowing they hadn't appealed to anyone, started to drift away.

"Hey, wait a moment!" Ah-xiu called them to a stop, then said to me, "Ask the Japanese to select a few more to join the fun. They're all so cute." Then she turned to the girls and shouted, "Just look at you—about as lively as bumps on a log. You don't laugh, you don't cry … you know, I'm not going to starve if you don't make anything, and I won't get fat if you do. I've got a bigger heart than any of you …"

Baba responded to the suggestion by saying there were already ten girls, including the three who had been assigned, and they didn't want any more. At this the girls started walking out of the room again. One of them grumbled as she passed through the door, "I could have told you they wouldn't want any more, so why did we have to stay behind and lose face … ?" I didn't hear the last part of the sentence, since she was walking out of the room as she said it, but Ah-xiu, who'd been helping inside, dropped what she was doing and ran after them.

"You bunch of tramps!" she screamed from the doorway. "You're a bunch of sluts!"

They asked me what Ah-x iu was yelling, but I couldn't translate that for them. All I said was, "She told them to have the kitchen hurry up with the food."

"Oh, I thought it was an argument. Japanese is still the best-sounding language, especially when spoken by women. It's just beautiful," said Ochiai proudly.

"That's for sure," agreed Sasaki. "Plenty of foreigners feel that way. How about you, Huang *kun*? "The others were nodding in agreement.

I'm afraid that even if an enlightened Japanese were to come to visit Taiwan, one of his ex-colonies, it would still be difficult to keep from exposing his feelings of superiority. How much more so then for Baba and the others of his generation, who come here, do what they please , attain their goals with money, whore around with our countrywomen, and even make fun of our language! With a forced gentleness to my voice, I said, "That's right, the Japanese language is just like your packaging designs—very attractive. Japanese has a nice sound to it, but its application is a whole different matter."

I stopped and looked at them for a moment. I could tell they didn't understand what I was trying to say. I was about to explain myself when another idea came to me; I said jokingly, "There's another facet to the Japanese language: take, for instance, sexual intercourse. Here in the countryside the people use the word 'screw,' while our soldiers say 'shoot your wad,' both of which you feel lack elegance and sound simply awf ul. But if you say 'have sex' in Japanese, or just use the foreign term that has been imported and swallowed whole, '*meiku rabu*' (make love), you think it's elegant and romantic-sounding."

I could see this struck them as funny, so I continued, "But

in fact, with 'screw,' 'shoot your wad,' 'have sex,' or '*meiku rabu*,' aren't we dealing with the same thing? Can it be that if you say '*meiku rabu*' you're talking about doing it differently somehow? Or maybe it lends the act respectability? Or perhaps it means that you can join bodies and souls as one and rise to the heights of supreme bliss?"

At first I had secretly reminded myself to sound as friendly as possible, but as I went along I grew more excited until I couldn't hold back. Fortunately the only parts of my discourse they paid any attention to were the vulgarities and the humor, so they laughed even harder. I didn't think it was all that funny, and it suddenly occurred to me that this analogy should not be used to criticize the Japanese language. It should be used as a criticism of the ego-pleasing and phony conduct of the intellectuals. When I saw that they'd mistaken my intent, treating my comments as a laughing matter, I felt uneasy. But something inside told me to just drop the matter.

When the food arrived, the topics of conversation began to expand. The girls sat down beside the men and started pouring wine and serving food to their customers. The girl with the tattoo, who had been standing the farthest from the room, was now sitting beside me and seeing to my needs enthusiastically. It occurred to me that I had a moral responsibility here, since her friendly attitude toward me had sprouted at a moment when her self esteem was at its lowest and I'd said, "I want you. Now won't you come in?" She had been moved by that. For someone like me who feels keen hostility toward Japanese, having to play the pimp in order to keep my job, making arrangements for them to whore around with my own countrywomen, had created immense inner conflicts. If I hadn't had the capacity to mask my feelings with a happy exterior—like a clown—I'm sure I couldn't have withstood the bitter struggle. Under conditions like these, how could I have any desire for a woman?

My heart cried out with the injustice of it all. If I didn't have her come to me that night, she would feel slighted; even though she was a prostitute, if I disappointed her after my actions had stirred up her emotions—even if it were only a one-night stand—I'd be guilty of trifling with her. I turned and looked at her. She returned my look shyly, then turned her face away again in what seemed to be a manifestation of her inferiority complex. Seeing how simple and unworldly she was, I didn't have the heart to disappoint her. *Okay, we'll see what happens tonight.*

A while earlier, before the other girls had come in, I'd interpreted the exchange between the first three girls—Xiaowen, Yingying, and Ahyu—and the men, and I was fed up with the role. Suddenly I had an inspiration: I'd open a provisional language course to teach the Japanese some Chinese and the girls some Japanese. But I'd only teach them the words for "good," "no good," "yes," and "no," and they could all learn them together. As soon as I mentioned my plan, they promptly agreed, and within three or four minutes had mastered their lessons. They were having a great time : a constant, uninterrupted flow of "yes," "no," "good," "no good" emerged from their mouths until they got so noisy I found it hard to continue my own conversation. I stood up, clapped my hands loudly, and shouted everyone down.

"Okay, now," I said, "you can say the words. From now on, communicate verbally and with hand and body language. Please, I beg you, don't bother me anymore." Things really began to heat up then. Even the most taciturn among them decided to try their hand, and as a result, whether they were getting through to each other or not, this became entertainment to go with their food and drink. The sounds of laughter alternately rose and fell, and even I was laughing so hard my sides were splitting. The girl on the other side of me said to Ochiai, "You're a son of a bitch."

"Good, good." Ochiai nodded vigorously to show how happy this made him. The girl, whose name was Meimei, was so overcome by laughter she collapsed over onto me. Ochiai asked me what she'd said. "Didn't you just say 'good'?" I asked. He said he guessed that what Meimei said must certainly have been interesting.

"It most assuredly was," I said. "She said you were a little chubby, but cute."

Ochiai was so happy he grabbed Meimei's hand and said, "Really? Hee hee hee, you're pretty cute yourself." There were many more of these comical exchanges, until soon they all began to suspect that they were being had and I was once again interpreting every word.

"Hey, friends," I said to the Japanese with a smile, "treat me like a human being too, all right? I can't just sit here and watch you have a good time, can I?" I reached over and put my arms around Ah-zhen, the girl with the tattoo, to give her a hug. Then I held out my wine cup and said, "I'll drain this cupful to express my apologies to you gentlemen." So saying, I drained the cup.

"Won't that make things difficult for us?" Baba asked good-naturedly.

"How could it? Doesn't your 'Thousand Beheadings Club' roam the world relying only on your swords?"

"Huang *kun*, you're the wittiest person we've met among the locals. We're no match for you."

"You flatter me." I picked up my wine cup again. "Here, let

this represent my gratitude for your flattering remarks." Again I drained the cup.

I could sense that from our first meeting at the airport till now their attitude toward me, or at least insofar as their speech and their conduct reflected it, had undergone quite a transformation. By this time they no longer exhibited any sense of superiority in front of me, and even Baba seemed a little intimidated by my presence.

As I observed them at the meal, I could see they were no longer inhibited by the language barrier, had turned it into a form of entertainment. And the knowledge that they were in a foreign country made them feel as if they were floating on air. Then they began to get the itch. Squinting his eyes and holding Qiuxiang in his arms, Baba said, "Huang *kun*, I'm afraid we can't avoid imposing upon you now. Do you know their price?"

I asked Ah-zhen, but she only stammered and was unable to say anything. Eventually, the girl sitting next to Tanaka, Baimei, was pushed forward by the others to speak for them.

"Are you interested in a 'rest' or a 'mooring'?" she asked. Actually, she had no idea of the real significance of the Japanese words *kyukei* and *teihaku*, which were remnants from the Japanese occupation. In this context, a "rest" meant a short time, and a "mooring" meant an overnighter.

"How much for a 'mooring'?"

"It's like this: if it's one of our own people, it's two hundred." Then she looked at the Japanese and asked softly, "They really don't understand what we're saying?"

"Not a word. Say anything you want as loudly as you like."

Nonetheless she continued in a low voice, "For Japanese it's four hundred."

"All right." Then in a loud voice I said, "We'll make it a thousand for a 'mooring.'"

"Hey, not so loud!" one of the girls blurted out. The others laughed.

"How much of it do we have to give you?" Baimei asked.

"None."

"How could we allow that?" several of them asked in unison.

"Don't worry about it." Then I said in Japanese, "One thousand for the night, and that's not a bad price. You can use your revalued yen and enjoy both convenience and economy."

"All right, let's decide." Baba nodded to the others with his head cocked to one side, indicating that he was asking for their opinions, although the inference was that he'd already made the decision for them.

"Baba *kun*, you still haven't asked Huang *kun* to take care of the arrangements for our trip to Hualien, have you?"

"Oh, I almost forgot," Baba said, striking himself on the forehead. "Huang *kun*," he said to me, "I'm going to have to ask another favor of you. We've heard that in Hualien you can find real aboriginal girls …" "I'm not sure," I answered calculatedly.

"You really don't know? Heh, heh, heh …" Ochiai asked teasingly.

"It doesn't make any difference. Huang *kun*, we plan to stay in Taiwan for a week, and Hualien is one of the places we want to visit. Call your company and have someone buy eight tickets for tomorrow's noon flight."

"Don't you mean seven tickets?" I asked.

"The eighth one is for you."

"I'm afraid I'll be busy tomorrow."

"Don't you want to come along with us?"

"It's not that. I really have things to do. But don't worry, if I can't make it, the company will send someone else to accompany you. Okay, I'll make the phone call," I said as I walked off.

"Sorry to trouble you."

When I returned to the room after making the call, nearly all the girls had left. Only Yingying and Xiaowen had stayed behind to clear the table.

"What's up? Where is everyone?" I asked.

"We asked them to leave for a while so we could make our preparations," Ochiai said with a mysterious grin. "Huang *kun*, how about you?"

"What preparations would I have to make?" I had an inkling of what he meant. I smiled, and Ochiai and the others smiled back.

"What about the phone call?"

"The plane takes off at 12:30. We'll leave here in the morning on the 9:31 train."

"Fine, no problem." Baba looked at the others. "That's it then."

Ochiai reached into his pocket and pulled out a little gold object that looked like a lipstick, only slightly larger. "Ever see one of these?"

I took it from him and opened it up. They were all standing around snickering as I examined it.

"A cologne atomizer?" I asked, putting my thumb on the button.

"Hey! Don't press it!" Ochiai yelled. "Don't press it!" They laughed.

"What is it anyway?" I hadn't a clue.

"Haven't you ever heard of the magic oil of India?"

"No."

Yingying and Xiaowen, thinking it was a cosmetic of some

sort, dropped what they were doing to come over and take a look. "What's that?" Xiaowen asked.

"Hey! Don't tell them." Ochiai grabbed it away from me, but then he must have remembered that they couldn't understand what he was saying. When he continued, he appeared to relish talking about it with them present so as to add some spice to the drama. He said, "An hour before we get to work, we spray a little of this stuff on the turtle's head—just a little. There's nothing like this stuff—the pleasure it brings is almost endless!" He smiled lecherously at the girls. "You know what I mean?"

Xiaowen reached over to take it, but I snatched it away. "This is an ointment for aches and pains," I said to her. "Hurry up and clear away the dishes." The girls walked away disappointed.

"Huang *kun*, you can try a little if you'd like," Baba said.

"I don't think so," I said, handing it back to Ochiai. I experienced a strange sort of anger.

"Huang *kun* isn't like us, he's still young. He probably doesn't need it."

By then they'd finished the food and wine, so they headed back to their rooms, to make their so-called preparations, I suspect. I went back to my room and lay down on the bed to sort out my feelings. My thoughts went around and around without ever coming together. Then they turned to Ah zhen, the girl with the tattoo . I was sure that if I summoned her that evening, she'd be happy to come and would be nicely submissive. Beginning to get aroused, I abruptly recalled that I'd be doing it along with the Japanese, and my anger was rekindled. *Should I not call her then? As self-debasing and simple as she is, she must certainly think that I want her tonight. If I don't call her she'll be hurt, and this hurt will go beyond just the missed chance to earn some money.* I thought and thought about it. *Damn it, I'll wait till tonight and see what happens!* Just as I was lying there feeling miserable, Baba knocked on the door and came in.

"Excuse me, Huang *kun*, sorry to disturb you."

Whatever the situation, they were always polite and courteous. But I was still disgusted with him. Once politeness and courtesy become habits and lose their spontaneity, what you're left with is blatant superficiality. He grinned as he said, "Can we call the girls now?"

"Now?" I sat up.

Baba nodded. I glanced at my watch.

"But it's only a little after six o'clock!" I said.

My startled reaction seemed to cause him some embarrassment. "You're right," he said with a smile, "it is a little early, but we've finished our preparations."

"You mean you've already sprayed on your magic oil of India?" Though there was a smile on my face, I wasn't feeling very happy.

He nodded. "And some other stuff as well. You see, since the potions are effective only for a period of time …" The smile on his face suddenly retreated and was replaced with a pathetic look.

"They don't have any side effects, do they?" My expression of concern was a complete fabrication.

"Of course they do, if you use them too often. But think about it—we're all in our fifties, and a thousand 'beheadings' is no simple task." As he said this, the last trace of a smile disappeared completely.

I stood up and patted him on the shoulder. "All right," I said, "I'll go."

"I'll be in my room." The smile he'd entered with started to make its return. But I knew that their smiles were dependent on the support they received from the magic oil of India and other stuff.

I walked out of my room against my own inclinations. Had there been someone behind me forcing me on, no matter how strong his arms, I'd have surely turned back to resist even if I were to die in the attempt. But when I turned back, there wasn't a thing in sight, and in that blur of time the cold, still corridor-almost deathlike—gave me a fright. In that fleeting moment I seemed to have moved from a strange and distant place back to reality. Unwilling though I was, I had no choice but to walk downstairs. At the desk at the foot of the stairs I ran into Ah-x iu, who had been serving us just a while before.

"Huang *san*," she addressed me in Japanese style, "what can I do for you?"

I was momentarily speechless, for I suddenly realized that I could not avoid asking her to have the girls go straight away to sleep with those Japanese. A while earlier, when I was negotiating the price, I hadn't felt so keenly what I was involved in, since I was able to more than double the going rate. In fact, I even experienced the stirrings of national consciousness—the illusion of serving my fellow Chinese. Whether or not such behavior and feelings were justified, I still experienced the thrill of dealing a defeat to my enemy. But not at this moment. As I stood there before Ah-xiu, I knew with absolute clarity that the moment I opened my mouth to speak, I'd be a bona fide pimp. "Damn it! Those Japanese want the girls to come to their rooms now," I said to her, showing my anger.

"Huh! Now? They can't go now. Why, it's only... what time is it?" She looked up at the clock on the wall, then at the girl behind the counter. "It's only six o'clock. How can they go now? Our girls aren't here to serve them alone."

"I know that, damn it! But …" I couldn't finish.

"We're not trying to take advantage of anyone," Ah-xiu said, "but the general rule is that a 'mooring' is from midnight on."

"We can't do that. No one expects a girl to spend the night starting this early," added the girl behind the counter.

"That's right! I know that," I said.

"Tell you what. I'll have the girls go up half an hour early, at eleven-thirty. How will that be?"

"That'd be fine, of course, except …" I paused for a moment. "Would you go upstairs with me and tell them personally? Just tell them what the general rule is."

"You'll have to be my interpreter."

As we walked upstairs, Ah-xiu said to me, "The girls here say you're a good guy." After a pause, she added, "Aren't you originally from Chiaohsi?"

"Who said so?" I answered with a start.

"Your home is next to the temple, and you're Uncle Yanlong's eldest son. Am I right?" She smiled.

"How did you know?"

"All the older people in our place recognized you."

"Uh-oh!"

"It doesn't matter." Then she asked me in a very lighthearted tone, "Did you go to Taipei right after you quit teaching? What sort of business are you in now? You must be doing well."

"Not really. I just work for a company."

"It's been years already, but Yumei still talks about you. She says you were the best teacher she ever had."

I stopped in my tracks and asked in a trembling voice, "Who's Yumei?"

"My eldest daughter. You were her fifth- and sixth-grade teacher." I remembered her and suddenly felt somewhat relieved.

"Oh! So Chen Yumei is your daughter! Where is she now?"

"She's in her first year at a girls' high school. She's changed quite a bit since you knew her. She's tall, taller even than me."

"Mrs. Chen, I have a favor to ask. Please don't tell Yumei I came here," I said awkwardly.

Mrs. Chen thought this was pretty funny. "I won't, but what difference would it make?" "No, please. Just say you ran into me somewhere—anywhere."

"I won't tell, I won't breathe a word," she said with a giggle.

We talked for a while longer at the head of the stairs. I still felt a slight heaviness in my heart, though I was more at ease than when Chen Yumei's mother first told me she knew who I was.

I took Mrs. Chen to find Baba and informed him of what she had told me.

"So that's how it is!" he said. "What a damned nuisance."

"I'm terribly sorry, but those are the rules around here." Mrs. Chen nodded apologetically.

"How about this, then: suppose we throw in a little more money, could we have them come now?"

"I'm sure that would be all right, but it might not be worth it."

I asked how much more each one would have to give for the girls to come now.

"At least two hundred."

"Let's tell them five hundred. After all, the Japanese are so rich they won't miss a few hundred."

After I informed Baba, he said, "Well, if that's how it is, we have no choice. I'll ask the others."

He knocked on each of the doors and called the others out

into the corridor; once they were all together he opened the discussion. When they arrived at their decision, Baba represented them. "I guess that's how it has to be. Huang *kun*, tell them to come right away." When it came to business and money, the Baba who had up to that moment given me the impression of someone who treated others politely had been transformed into a person just like everyone else.

Before long, all the girls they had requested, excepting Xiuxiu, whom Takeuchi had wanted, arrived in the rooms. Mrs. Chen and I took the thoroughly displeased Takeuchi downstairs to the resting quarters to select another girl who appealed to him. After the longest time he grudgingly settled on a girl named Meijun. It seemed to me that my conduct had been abruptly and severely restricted ever since Mrs. Chen had told me that most of the people in the hotel knew me. I experienced an unremitting anxiety: had I said or done anything out of line in the presence of my fellow villagers? *Damn it, I'm here with Takeuchi, picking out a girl as if she were a piece of goods.* He continued the process a while longer. By rights I should have been doing something for the girl, but seeing the exasperated look on Takeuchi's face, I stood frozen off to the side, embarrassed to death.

After Takeuchi walked off with Meijun, Mrs. Chen came up behind me. "How about you, Huang *san*?" she asked with a smile. She had the best of intentions; if I'd wanted the company of a girl, she wouldn't have thought anything of it, working as she did in such a place. But her smile brought me unbearable discomfort. I knew what she had in mind.

"No, not for me, thanks."

"You don't have to be so straitlaced. Ninety percent of those who take it on the chin are straitlaced people."

Hai! I had to laugh inwardly. *God knows if I'm an honest man!*

But all I said was, "That's all right. This has nothing to do with being straitlaced or not."

She laughed and let the matter drop as she followed me upstairs. Naturally, that took me by surprise, since I'd hoped she'd press the issue, giving me the opportunity to ask her advice on how to handle the matter of Ah-zhen, the girl with the tattoo.

"Mrs. Chen," I said, pausing at the bend in the staircase, "I'm sure Ah-zhen is under the impression that I want her this evening. But actually ..."

"Don't you worry about it. I'll find a nice girl for you."

She'd misunderstood me. Of course, I'm no saint, but in my complex and totally self-contradictory state of mind I couldn't come up with a single decent idea.

"No. I'd like to give her five hundred and not have her come to my room tonight."

"That's not necessary. I'll tell her and it'll be all right."

"But I ... I made arrangements with her earlier." This was the best way to handle it. If I were to say I was fearful of injuring Ah-zhen's self-respect and adding to her low opinion of herself, Mrs. Chen might laugh at me, I thought. At the same time, I was terribly afraid of running into Ah-zhen. I took five hundred dollars out of my pocket and gave it to her.

"If that's how you want it, you don't have to give so much. One hundred is plenty." She kept one of the bills and gave me four back.

I took three and handed back one. "How's this? Give her two hundred."

"Ha ha! She makes a hundred percent profit, just like that," she said with a laugh as she took the money.

I went back to my room, lay down, and stared blankly at the ceiling. I had nothing to look forward to but a long evening alone in my room, and I didn't know what to do with myself. How could I go to sleep so early in the day?

Since I'd been away for a long time, I thought about going home to have a look around. But Father would ask me when I'd arrived and what I'd come home for. If I told him the truth, that I was accompanying some Japanese on a pleasure excursion to Chiao-hsi ... ai! I wouldn't even try. I'd only be looking for trouble. Years earlier, when I'd chosen not to take over his brokerage and even quit my job as a teacher, a scene had erupted that had left a lingering bad taste. If I were to tell him now that the job I'd gone to Taipei for was bringing Japanese here to the hot springs to whore around, nothing I could say would make any difference; even plunging into the Yellow River could not wash the stains away.

I didn't want to dwell on it any longer. There was no going home!

Instead, I thought of other places I could go. But wouldn't it be the same? If I ran into any friends, wouldn't they ask my reasons for coming home? They might even let my father know, and things would be even worse. To travel to Chiao-hsi and not even come home! It would be like two years ago, when he'd screamed, "When the ancient sage emperor Yu was taming the Yellow River, he passed by his home three times without entering. But you! Who the hell do you think you are?" If he were to fly into another rage because of me, this time he might die of apoplexy. No, that was no good either. I decided to just lie there.

I rolled over and noticed a photograph of a foreign pinup girl hanging on the wall. She was straddling a chair backwards and cradling her chin in a waiting pose. As I was looking at it my train of thought quickly turned in a new direction. I figured that those Japanese—*Damn them*—were just then reaching their climaxes.

I wondered what effects the magic oil of India had. Who knows, if I hadn't been recognized by Yumei's mother, maybe Ah-zhen would already be lying beside me. There's a saying men have: "Ugly women are great in bed."

With her low opinion of herself and my expression of interest in her, I'm sure she'd have shown me a terrific time. *Damn it! I wonder what she's doing right now.* But no matter how overcome by my own desires I was, something inside me maintained awareness. It was this that kept me from daring to face myself, and the less I dared to do that, the fewer my chances of escape. As a result, I felt ill at ease and so pained that I jumped violently to my feet. I lit a cigarette and paced the floor. Suddenly I noticed the telephone. I reached out and took it off the hook; the girl at the desk answered.

"Front desk, may I help you?"

"Oh, I'm sorry, it was nothing." I hung up. But I was immediately aware that what I'd just done was very unusual, and if the girl at the desk were to mention it later to anyone—especially Yumei's mother—it would be the object of a lot of speculation, and even my private thoughts would become common knowledge. Ai! More cause for embarrassment! I figured the best thing to do would be to leave my tiny room.

I went downstairs, apologized to the girl at the counter, then went into the restaurant, found a table, and ordered some food and a bottle of beer. I sat there trying to figure out what sort of lie I could tell my wife to avoid having her suspect me of being unfaithful. Thoughts that had sprung from my own imagination and those that had their origins elsewhere came to me one after another for some time. Eventually I was like a lonely long-distance runner undergoing slow and agonizing physical and mental torture: I finally reached the finish line, dead drunk and empty.

JAPAN'S LONGEST DAY

When I opened my eyes the following morning I saw Ah-xiu, Baba, and the others standing around my bed. In a dazed state of mind, I was shocked awake by the anxious looks on their faces and by their apprehensive comments. "Huang *kun*, there's nothing wrong, is there?" I sat up with a start.

"What's happened?" I asked.

"You scared us. We thought you were sick."

"No, I'm fine. Look!" I sat up and threw a couple of punches in the air. "There's nothing wrong."

They laughed. Then Mrs. Chen told me they'd knocked repeatedly without being able to awaken me. They couldn't even get me up by ringing my telephone. Finally, they'd asked her to bring the passkey.

"It's getting late," Baba said. "Didn't you say we'd be taking a train a little after nine o'clock?"

"Mrs. Chen, did you get the tickets for us?" I asked.

"Yes, the 9:31 train. I'll get them for you in a minute."

"Hm, 9:31." I looked at my watch. "There's no problem, we still have about an hour. The train station is close by." Then I said to Mrs. Chen in Taiwanese, "Will you get our bill ready, please? Have they paid the girls?"

"Yes."

I took out another two hundred and gave it to her as a tip. "My goodness, how embarrassing to be tipped by Teacher Huang. Thanks a lot," she said as she left.

"Huang *kun*, you must have had a great time last night, eh."

"Um, I had a good time." In matters of this kind, no one believes you if you say you didn't do anything. And even if you manage to convince them, you'll be laughed at and suffer a considerable loss of face. So it's better just to say yes.

"No wonder you couldn't get up," Baba said with a look of envy in his eyes. "You must have had quite a time—a night of pure enjoyment!"

I grinned at them, secretly pleased that these dimwits were so easy to fool.

"How about the rest of you?" I asked.

"Not bad!"

"Well, I didn't enjoy myself!"

A voice full of displeasure came from somewhere near the window behind me. The others were convulsed with laughter, but it took me aback. It was Takeuchi. He stood there looking out the window, keeping his back to us.

"What's the matter, Takeuchi *kun*?" I asked him.

"Go ahead, tell him. It won't hurt," Baba said.

Takeuchi turned around with a forced smile as Baba said with a laugh, "In the years since we founded our 'Thousand Beheadings Club,' we've made one discovery. Most people, maybe even you, would probably call it superstition, but what happens is that whenever one of us encounters bare skin…uh…a bare surface…" He grinned as he paused. "What I mean is, if he makes a girl without pubic hair, then unfortunate things begin to happen to him."

"Are you kidding?"

"Last year, after I had one in Hong Kong, I lost a thousand U.S. dollars. Ochiai had one, after which his factory burned down. Sasaki had an auto accident and spent two months in the hospital. And then there was …"

"That's enough!" Takeuchi interrupted.

"Yes, that's enough," I agreed. "Those are coincidences. You don't really believe in such superstitions, do you?"

As I was talking, I observed Ochiai looking for something in his bag. Happy as could be, he pulled out a little memo book with a red sateen cover, walked over, and flipped through the pages.

"Take a look at this," he said.

I took it from him and was startled when I realized what it was. I began to silently curse them. The little book, it turned out, was a record they kept for the "Thousand Beheadings Club." Each page recorded the time and place, the name of the girl, a description of her figure, how the lovemaking went, and what happened, followed by a critique. The bottom half of the page was left blank so they could use a piece of transparent tape to affix one of the girl's pubic hairs.

"Get it now?" Ochiai said with a grin. "Takeuchi's page for today won't …"

"All right, all right, I guess you're happy now!" Takeuchi shouted.

Why was he so angry? There was a lot I didn't know about their "Thousand Beheadings Club."

Later I learned that each of them had one of these little books, which they used to exchange experiences. If they made some sort of discovery this way, then everyone could perform experiments based upon it.

Once they were on the train they began discussing their experiences of the night before, holding nothing back.

"Hey!" I interrupted. "There are people all over Taiwan who speak better Japanese than I do, maybe right here beside us."

"We're not discussing politics or anything," Baba responded.

"I know you're not, but we Chinese aren't accustomed to talking about sex so openly and are embarrassed to hear such things in public places." I knew my words were a little inflammatory, but what the hell, those are the breaks! It wouldn't do any good to suppress my feelings any longer. But I still had a smile on my face.

They were speechless for a moment; then Baba said with a nervous laugh, "Huang *kun*, you're not angry, are you?"

I laughed and said, "How's that? If I were angry, I'd keep my mouth shut. It's just possible, however, that someone might be offended and come over with mayhem on his mind."

They were frightened by this prospect, at least a little, and after taking a look around they turned back to me.

"Could that really happen?" Sasaki asked softly.

"We don't have to worry about such things in Japan," said Ochiai. "But that's Japan—this is not Japan!" I said.

"Naturally," said Baba, "but I don't necessarily agree with Ochiai *kun*. In Japan we too ..." Obviously trying to salvage some dignity for his country, he quickly realized that he was on shaky ground, so he paused momentarily.

Ochiai picked up the conversation, saying with some displeasure, "Baba *kun*, is that really necessary?"

I returned to the attack, responding to what Baba had been about to say, remembering to keep a smile on my face.

"Baba *kun*, no matter what the situation, if there's something that embarrasses you in Japan or something you don't dare do for fear of injuring others, then you shouldn't do it when you go abroad, at least in regards to what we're talking about. Isn't that right?"

"No, hold on a moment, Huang *kun*, I didn't make myself clear. What I meant was ..."

"That's enough, Baba *kun*, that's just about enough. Let's

everybody speak for himself. Who asked you to be Japan's spokesman?" Then Tanaka said to me, "Huang *kun*, please don't be so sensitive. Heh, heh …"

I laughed along with him. "Tanaka *kun*, who's being sensitive? But you make it sound improper to be sensitive about things. Besides, since you're Japanese, under certain circumstances or in certain situations you can't avoid representing Japan. But I agree—everyone should speak for himself."

"You see! I said all along that Huang *kun* is the sharpest Taiwanese we've ever met, didn't I?" Baba said.

"Let's just forget it," I said. "And let's all take it easy."

"How can we take it easy now? Huang *kun*, you're really something. You created the tense situation, and now you want *us* to take it easy!"

"You've got it all wrong. But okay, do what you want." Then I added, "Don't worry about me. In case anything happens, I'll still be here beside you."

"Then we can put our minds at ease," Baba said.

But after my warning, they seemed to run out of things to say. They sat there like blocks of wood. I had no idea what they were thinking. When the train pulled into Ting-shuang-hsi, Ochiai asked, "How long before we get to Taipei?"

"Another hour."

"We still have that far to go?"

"Mm-hm."

A young man who'd evidently boarded at T'ou-ch'eng was standing near us. I noticed right off that he was tuned in to our conversation. I'd cautioned them not to talk about their sexual experiences on the train partly because I felt they were being too flagrant about it and partly because I'd noticed this young man who was engrossed in their comments. As our eyes met, he smiled and nodded. I nodded back.

"Excuse me, sir, you're Chinese, aren't you?"

"Yes, I am."

"It's hard to believe that someone as young as you can speak such fluent Japanese."*

"You're too kind. I barely manage."

"My name is Chen, and I'm a senior in the Chinese Department at Taiwan University. After I graduate, my father is going to find a way to send me to Japan for advanced study. So could I trouble you to ask these Japanese a few questions for me?"

Just as I was thinking to myself that he might be a little too brash, he asked abruptly, "What do those men do in Japan?"

Damn this young fellow! If I ask some of the questions he has in mind, they might laugh at the presumptuousness of our young people. Besides, isn't it all topsy-turvy for a student of Chinese literature to leave Taiwan and go abroad to do advanced study? Then I had an inspiration. Why not take this opportunity to hurl a few barbs at the Japanese and teach my young friend a lesson at the same time? The prospect of a little sport nearly made me laugh out loud. Serious though the matter at hand may have been, I figured this would be a good chance to have some fun.

I told the young man they were a fact-finding group of Japanese college professors.

"Oh, that's perfect!" He was delighted. "Would you mind helping me out?"

Though the others couldn't understand what we were saying, they were watching our expressions closely and with great concentration, especially when the young man was speaking.

---

* As a rule, only Taiwanese educated before 1945 speak Japanese fluently.

When I turned back to the Japanese, the young man nodded to them, and they timidly returned his gesture. "He's a college senior," I said. "His field is history, and since he's writing a thesis on the War of Resistance, he'd like to discuss a few things with some Japanese."

They were momentarily speechless. Then one of them said confidentially, "As businessmen, we don't know anything about that."

"That doesn't matter. Besides, I don't know what he's going to ask." I turned to him. "They'll be pleased to answer your questions, though they're afraid you might not find their answers satisfactory. Also, before you begin, they'd like to ask you something first. They want to know why someone studying Chinese literature would want to go to Japan to do research."

"I've heard there are lots of original editions there," he said. Uncomfortable with this answer, I felt like responding right then and there. But I kept my feelings in check and pretended to give his answer to the Japanese.

"He'd like to know if you were born around 1916," I said.

They looked at one another with shocked expressions, wondering how the young man could have guessed so accurately and why he seemed to be investigating them. Actually, I'd already learned this from registering them at the hotel.

"What does he want to know that for?" Baba asked with an expression of displeasure. "Huang *kun*, this can't have anything to do with the thesis he's writing. Besides, that's personal."

Seeing that the young man had observed the look of displeasure on Saba's face, I quickly told him, "Professor Baba is disappointed with your response, even a little upset. He said that research in any field of knowledge doesn't depend upon the edition one uses. For example, if you're doing work on the *Book of History*, using both an original and a later edition, will you gain a deeper understanding from the former?"

"But your mood and feelings while you're doing the research won't be the same. Also ..."

"Hold on there," I interrupted him. "If you say too much at one time, I won't be able to interpret for you, so let me tell them what you just said first." I turned to the Japanese. "He offers his apologies for asking this sort of question, but he wants to gain an understanding of the background of those days, that's all. He'll understand if you don't feel like answering him." Then, speaking for myself, I said, "Were you, as a matter of fact? What difference could telling him make?"

"Well, if that's all it is, actually, all seven of us were born in 1917. We're from the same town and we were classmates in elementary and high school." When Baba finished, the others stared intently while I spoke to the young man.

"Many people who do research in Chinese are under the impression that they're doing research on Chinese words. But what's really worth re searching is Chinese society and the great Chinese thinkers. He said that your wanting to go to Japan to do research in Chinese literature is actually just a pretext, isn't it?"

An embarrassed smile appeared on the young man's face. "No, it isn't. I really want to go to Japan to study. But what the professor says is certainly worth thinking about. Could I ask if he's a sinologist?"

"No, he's a professor of Japanese literature, but anyone in Japanese literature has a solid foundation in sinology." I was beginning to get a little flustered. I hoped I wouldn't forget what I was supposed to be asking the Japanese and wind up giving apple answers to questions about oranges.

"My papa's always telling me that Japan is a pretty good place, so I'd like to see it for myself."

Baba and the others were looking at me, waiting to hear what was being said. I turned to them. "He said you must have been just the right age to be drafted into the army and take part in the war of aggression against China, right?" I looked first at the pale face of Ochiai, then at the composed Baba. I said with a laugh, "This fellow doesn't care much for others' feelings. But there's no harm done. Ochiai *kun*, you seem a little touchier about this than the others. What's wrong?"

"Nothing's wrong." He paused for a moment, as if troubled. "In those days everybody but the disabled was drafted into the army. Naturally, we were no exception."

"A great war isn't caused by common folk. I don't care if you call it a war of aggression, because it was initiated by the Imperial Government in power. Me, I just followed orders." Baba looked at the others. "Isn't that right?"

"To listen to you now, you'd think that you opposed that war down to your marrow. But what about those days? Weren't you right in there singing about how you represented the Way of Heaven in its destruction of the unrighteous, marching onto the continent of China as you sang, and calling it a 'holy war?'" Then I forced a smile and said, "If I'd been in your shoes, I guess I'd have done the same."

Suddenly feeling as if a great weight had been lifted from their shoulders, they all laughed nervously.

"So you've been to the China mainland? When you were in the army, that is?"

"All except Takeuchi *kun*."

"I seem to have gotten interested in the subject myself, but actually these are his questions." I smiled, then turned to the student and said, "The professors hope you'll forgive them if they sometimes seem impolite by being critical of your thoughts in this matter."

"Oh, don't worry about that. I should be thanking them," he answered.

"They say it's understandable that your father has good feelings about Japan, because people of his age grew up under a Japanese educational system that kept them ignorant. But someone of your generation shouldn't have such thoughts."

"It was my papa who told me..."

"Let me finish. Professor Baba also said that supposing Japan is a fine place, or America is a fine place, or somewhere else is a fine place, what you seem to have in mind is to go to a fine place somewhere to enjoy yourself, or perhaps just to escape from reality. What he wants to ask you is this: granted that Japan is a fine place, just what have you done for Japan? If the answer is nothing, then you'd best not make plans to reap the benefits of her accomplishments." I smiled. "But the professor says this is just a personal reaction to your comments, and if you really want to go to Japan, he says you'd be welcome."

"I wouldn't go there just to have a good time! I'd go to study!"

"Going to study is fine, and that's your business. What the professor says is not intended as a criticism of you but is aimed at today's youth and their dissatisfaction with reality, which makes them all want to run off to a better country that exists only in their imagination. These are the people he's talking about. Only you know whether or not you're one of them."

"What he says is right, and I respect him for it. How many days will they be here looking things over? It would be wonderful if they could speak at our school."

I'll be damned! So this is what our young students have come to. It's the sort of common-sense talk you can hear anywhere, but in the mouth of a foreigner it somehow gains credibility. Hmm. "Only monks from afar really know the Scriptures!" Although it struck me as funny, it unnerved me a little as well. I'd started out wanting to poke a little fun; how could I have guessed that I'd soon be attacking both parties? I knew I didn't have enough under standing of these matters to keep it up forever, and sooner or later I'd slip up. I figured it was time to put on the brakes. But how? Since I didn't know, I decided to keep it up until the young man got off the train.

The strange part was, I hadn't expected that in using my limited knowledge of history to settle some accounts with the Japanese I'd actually induced these men with their superior airs to simply acknowledge a debt by slowly nodding their heads.

"This student has made his position clear, and I think we can accept it."

"I hope that in his thesis he won't use our viewpoint as a critique of Japan."

I was elated to hear Sasaki say this, for I could see how little remained of the pleasures they'd bought the night before. But I wasn't quite ready to let them off the hook yet. I wanted to turn their pleasure into anguish, no matter how ephemeral it might be. "I don't think he will," I said. "To draw general conclusions from an isolated situation is taboo in scholarly work. I'm sure a college student understands that."

"I hope so," Sasaki said. Then he continued, "Not long after the war, when TV came to Japan, we were finally able to witness the past in documentaries about the war we'd been involved in ...."

"Did you see any of the fighting in China?"

"Sure! Quite a bit, as a matter of fact." He looked at his friends. "Isn't that right? It was then that we were able to really see what kinds of things we'd done."

I feigned a confused expression. "How could you have a clear picture of what you'd done after seeing documentaries?"

"Oh!" Ochiai, his face looking drawn, showed signs of real discomfort .As for the others, although they exchanged glances, their attention never strayed from our conversation. Sasaki blurted out almost painfully, "We saw the rape of Nanking, we saw bodies floating on the Whampoo River, we saw the bombing, we saw ...."

"Sasaki *kun*, that's enough," Baba said, shaking his head, "that's enough, that's enough."

I agreed, he'd said enough. They'd been parties to it, and if they'd truly seen documentaries giving irrefutable proof of their ruthless persecution of the Chinese, there was no need for me to pursue the matter any further. This reminder that I'd given them was all any humane, conscionable human being could stand. Seeing the mental anguish written on their faces, I could tell I'd achieved the desired effect. But what could I say at this juncture to the young fellow beside me, who seemed so terribly eager to know what was going on?

I continued having my sport with both parties for a while longer.

"Young fellow, please don't be angry."

"I won't."

"Just now they wanted to ask you something else. You told them you'd never been to the Palace Museum; that came as quite a shock. And a real disappointment. You say you're a college student and that your major subject is Chinese, that you even live in Taipei. Then why haven't you taken the time to go have a look?" I could see he was still swallowing the bait; he lowered his head slightly with an expression of shame. "They said that even though they're in Taiwan for a visit of only a few days, they've already been to the museum twice. They said their minds have been troubled as they wonder how a magnificent race of people that was able to produce the cultural treasures in the museum could in recent years have dried up so completely."

"Mr. Huang, I'm so ashamed."

"But then, you're too honest. When you meet foreigners who are so concerned about China, you should lie and say you've been to the museum. And if that sort of thing embarrasses you, then why not just go there someday and take a look for yourself? But no matter, what's happened today is no real loss of face—at least you're sincere. But isn't there something you'd like to ask them about Japan? Before you could even start, their questions kept you from asking them anything."

"I did have some questions, but after listening to what they've said, my questions don't seem so important any longer. I feel this has been a lucky day for me—I've learned at lot."

"As a matter of fact, you can hear people right here saying the things they were telling you today. It's strange: if your own people say something it's a fart in the wind, but if a foreigner says the same thing it's a message from the gods. Isn't that right?"

"But honestly, I've never heard any of this before."

"Sure, I know. I'm saying that it happens a lot."

I glanced over at the Japanese; they were sitting there as if they were about to hear a judge pronounce a sentence. When I turned to talk to them, they changed their posture slightly to concentrate on what I was saying.

"I hope you'll forgive this brash young man …" I didn't have a chance to finish.

"What do you mean? We couldn't respect him more!"

"Youngsters his age are on the romantic side and generally more patriotic. I already told him not to ask any more questions, since it's all history anyway. You've come here to enjoy yourselves, and talking about the past like this can only cause you unhappiness." I paused for a moment. "But he did say that after the Japanese put down their weapons, they switched to economic aggression, where they don't have to see their victims' suffering. I told him he shouldn't say that, but he said it is economic aggression, and from certain angles…"

"Huang *kun*, that's enough," Baba said, shaking his head, "that's enough!"

Sasaki said agonizingly, "Huang *kun*, I'm so sorry."

"Why should you be?" I said with a smile.

"We all feel very guilty. Please tell this young man how much we respect him. If the postwar Japanese youths were at all like him, I think there'd be hope for our country." From the very beginning I could sense that Sasaki was more deeply affected than the others. The situation this time, in which their reveries had caused such pain, had started with him and spread to the others.

The train pulled to a stop at Pa-tu. The young man broke in on our conversation.

"Mr. Huang, this is my station. Thank you, thank you all." He bowed to me and to the others. This so unnerved the Japanese that they jumped to their feet and returned his courtesies, almost as if they had received a great favor.

"This is where he gets off," I said.

"*Sayonara!*" It never occurred to me that the young fellow knew a word or two of Japanese. This was the first time I hadn't mediated their conversation. They were actually communicating with each other.

"*Zaijian!*" Nor had I suspected that these Japanese had learned to say a word or two of Chinese. Each of them shook hands very gravely with the young man as they parted.

"*Sayonara.*"

"*Zaijian.*"

The young man left, and they all sat down. Sasaki, deeply moved, sighed. "There's a Chinese youth you can be proud of."

"And how about me?" I asked playfully.

There was a hint of returning smiles as they said, "You too, naturally."

God only knows! This struck me as pretty funny.

"I was right, wasn't I? You have to mind what you say in public. If that young man had understood Japanese, things wouldn't have turned out as they did."

"Huang *kun*," said Baba, "let's not talk about it anymore."

They leaned back languidly against their seats. Ochiai asked, "Huang *kun*, how much longer?"

"About thirty minutes."

"Still thirty minutes to go?" he blurted out, as if the remaining half hour of our trip would take forever.

1973

Bright Red Shrimps—
An Anecdote about Limp Dick Le-zai

A place called Guiliao-zai.
A young man walks home with a plow over his shoulder at dusk after the work is done in the field. He puts the plow down to take a break along the way, causing his father, who is driving their ox in front, to turn and say, "What a Limp Dick Le-zai! The plow is crushing you, is that it?"

A young woman has just finished plucking bristles off a pig's foot. Her mother-in-law walks over, picks it up, and turns it over in her hand before tossing it back into a washbasin. "Yo! What a Limp Dick Le-zai! No one would trade a pair of logan pits for your eyes."

A group of village children are playing with a spinning top on the temple grounds. One of them flings it to the ground but isn't able to pick it back up before it goes outside the circle drawn in the dirt. Smacking himself on the back of his head with a look of shame on his face, he reproaches himself: "Ah—I'm a real Limp

Dick Le-zai."

And so it went. It hadn't been long, barely two decades, in fact, since Limp Dick Le-zai had become synonymous with stupid, good-for-nothing, worthless, useless, and trash in Guiliao-zai, where the common expression became part of the village culture.

Huang Dingle of Guiliao-zai had come down with a serious kidney problem some two decades earlier and turned into a completely different man. He had been called Ah-le-zai before the illness; the villagers added Limp Dick to his name afterward. Now he was known as Limp Dick Le-zai. How had this happened? Or, to put it a different way, what would cause a man to suffer from the complications of this problem? Older folks in the village had a variety of explanations. Some said it was caused by having sex with a menstruating woman; others claimed it was because he'd had sex with a woman during the lying-in period. A more superstitious reason had to do with the filth of sex violating the sanctity of a temple. In any case, it seemed to be closely connected to an overindulgence in sex. When a man has too much sex, he will be afflicted with underactive kidneys and a loss of potency. Without timely care, that will result in kidney malfunction and the total depletion of male essence and vitality, eventually leading to Limp Dick problems, a complete loss of the yang.

In retrospect, every adult in the village thought that for Ah-le-zai it had been inevitable. First of all, they believed it was quite possible that some sexual filth had indeed violated a temple, because the village's King of Five Grains Temple was directly opposite Huang Dingle's house. He could have sex ten thousand times, but it would only take once to break the taboo if a cat, a dog, a chicken, or a duck suddenly acted up and he chased the creature out of the house right after sex. Secondly, it seemed to have become an ironclad, irrefutable fact that either he'd had sex with a woman who was menstruating or in the lying-in period, or he was oversexed. Once during a chat, someone made a rough calculation of the age differences between the six sons borne by Ah-le's wife. The second was only a year younger than his brother; the third and fourth weren't twins but were barely a year apart, since the third was born in the first month and the fourth in the last month of the same year. The fifth and sixth came into this world in similar temporal fashion. Which meant that Auntie Ah-le's womb had never been idle for longer than two months out of a year, and it could have been busier if he hadn't come down with the problem. It was clear to everyone that her belly had been full and then empty once every year, in and out, like the rhythmic breathing of a healthy person.

Back then, before he was afflicted with his problem, he often thumped his chest to brag about his prowess when the conversation among a group of men turned to sex. He made the others wish they could get some action, and they looked at him enviously. But he changed into a different man, inside and out, once he began suffering from his problem, and he no longer spoke with a powerful voice. He lost interest in an ambitious plan to dig a pond downstream of the creek to raise turtles, as if it had never crossed his mind. Naturally, he had to give up major undertakings, but even small jobs were beyond his ability. Take the tiny mouse hole in the bedroom's brick wall, for example. Every winter, a cold northern wind blew in through the hole, and the parts of his body outside the blanket would get so cold they'd turn numb. He often thought about mixing a lump of clay with cow dung to patch the hole, but the northern wind had come and gone each year and nothing had happened, not even the simple solution of filling the hole with straw. The mouse hole had indeed turned into a moon gate, as the saying goes.

In the past, he had loved to show off his virility by asking someone to push a carrying pole against his belly, but now his body had fallen apart; his handsome straight back had become bowed, and his hard, sculpted muscles had lost their definition. His physique was more like the curling outer leaves of a cabbage with the advent of the time period known as White Dew. Huang Dingle was saddened by the sorry sight of his shriveled maleness when he took a bath; he decided not to look at it again, filled with the bitterness and resentment of a father who has lost hope for a worthless son and refuses to set his eyes on the prodigal child. He merely splashed on some water when he got to that part of his anatomy during his bath. But he might have hurt its feelings too much, for he developed a case of eczema, which required his special attention, no matter how disappointed he was in that worthless organ. His special care, however, was intended simply to ease his physical suffering, and he had no real feeling for it. When the problem first occurred, he felt that all the fun and enjoyment had gone out of his life. He was embittered by the situation, so he naturally hated his nickname, but he felt that even his actual name on the household registry put him to shame, so he turned it into an adversary. The name Huang Dingle (utter happiness) was too glaring to his eyes, harsh to his ears, and damaging to his feelings. He couldn't get away from his name no matter where he went, even if he could hide from others' jeering mockery.

Yet his torment paled in comparison to what his wife was going through. The men in the village all said it was hard for a woman to be a widow, but even harder to be a grass widow who could look but not enjoy. To cure his problem, she had run from village to village and sought out every single doctor. In terms of remedies, they had exhausted all the possibilities; Ah-le-zai even ate a puppy when that was rumored to be effective. He had tried all the yang-restoring tonics, from horned toads to deer penises. When it came to divination and asking for divine intervention, they prayed to Naza, the celestial prince, and Laozi, the supreme king, they drew divination sticks, and they cast trigrams. Anything would send her off on an earnest and tireless search, as long as it offered a shred of hope. There could be a typhoon outside, but she would run around, in and out, like a horse with five hooves; in the process she had used up quite a bit of the clan's communal purse, drawing ire and gossip from some female relatives. Ah-le-zai was often in the dark about what she was doing, for the women showed their fangs only in front of her.

One time she used all her private savings to pay for a pricey herbal remedy and secretly made a medicinal tea. She brought it to him in bed and, knowing he was irritable after years of suffering, offered cautiously, "Drink it while it's hot."

He stared blankly at the ceiling, silent and unmoving.

"Hurry. Once the medicine cools off, it will lose its power and become less effective. Come on," she said.

Finally he reacted, though only to exhale slowly.

"What else can we do?" She laid the bowl on the edge of the bed. "What's the point of getting upset?" She told herself that she should be the one getting angry. She'd been forced to endure a prolonged exchange filled with hurtful and upsetting words earlier that morning when she was doing laundry with some female kin by the well. Ah-ye, the wife of the oldest son, had said to Ah-mi, the wife of the second son, "Whose pants are those? They're like rags."

"They're Ah-tong's. What can I do? The clan account is running low," Ah-mi said as she held up the pants and gave them a shake. The women exchanged a look before glancing at Ah-le's wife.

"Don't be ridiculous. There must be money for a pair of pants even if the account is running low. I would never let that stop me. Go buy a pair for Ah-tong tomorrow. I'm going to buy something for Ah-ji as well."

Ah-ye took a pair of pants out of her laundry basket. "Look. These are pretty bad, too, though they're not as worn as Ah-tong's."

"Oh, they are really tattered, more like a rag," Ah-mi said in an exaggerated show of agreement. "But our mother-in-law won't agree. Even her clothes have seen better days."

"I don't care. We have to work together and make our demands."

"Unless our men also suffer from Limp Dick problems," Ah-mi said with a smile.

Unable to take it any longer, Ah-le's wife put down the clothes in her hands and looked up at them. Their eyes met, but the staring contest quickly yielded a winner when Ah-le's wife lowered her head.

Ah-ye broke the silence and said in a lighthearted tone, "Everyone says it takes two coins to make a sound. If a woman doesn't overdo it, why would the man be like that?"

"You're right. We're women, too, aren't we?"

Ah-le's wife was so outraged she felt the blood rush to her head. It was all she could do to keep from slapping them. Naturally, though, that was just a thought, since she was no match for Ah-ye when it came to squabbling, let alone a real fight. Ah-ye's mouth was like a machine gun, and Ah-le's wife would never forget a bitter defeat at the other woman's hand. She couldn't walk away, either, because she hadn't finished the pile of clothes; worse yet, they would have a great time at her expense if she left. She could tell them she'd stopped using the clan money, but that wouldn't help. The source of her private money would, in Ah-ye's mouth, turn into something they could hold over her forever. The only thing she could do was make enough noise while scrubbing and pounding the clothes to drown out their voices.

She wanted to tell Ah-le what had happened that morning, so he would understand how much she suffered because of him and would drink the brew. But she had second thoughts, caused by a different concern. Ah-le hated to hear her complain about what Ah-ye and Ah-mi did. As a matter of fact, he had been wary of Ah-ye's big mouth to begin with, and now his unsavory illness could only provoke her into more humiliating rants. After some calm consideration, Ah-le's wife was able to sort out the complicated relationship and gain a better perspective, so she hid her unhappiness and repeated patiently, "Drink it now. Hurry. It's getting cold. It'd be a shame to waste it."

He sat up looking irritated. She quickly steadied the bowl so he wouldn't knock it over.

"One mouthful is all it takes. Come on, finish it."

"Finish it? Do you think my stomach is a medicine cabinet? Tell me, how much have I already had?"

"But it's for your own good."

"I don't need it." He pushed the bowl away from his lips, spilling half of its contents. His action brought out all her unhappiness and sense of injustice, and she put the bowl down on the edge of the bed, covered her face with her hands, and began to sob bitterly. She said in a muffled voice, "I should die, I know. I ought to die. When I'm dead, you'd be—"

Ah-le was mad at himself for making her cry, realizing how much she had suffered recently. *Damn, what a stupid woman. What exactly is she giving me? Is that a magic potion or some secret remedy? Why didn't she tell me how much it cost before putting the bowl up to my lips?* He stole a glance at his wife, and then at the remaining liquid in the bowl. *Maybe this one will work,* he said to himself. The strong aroma of the tonic suddenly made him aware of its potential power, and he felt an irrepressible desire to drink it down. Yet he knew he had to adjust his attitude before approaching the bowl when he recalled his earlier reaction.

His wife, who had had her fair share of suffering, was so overwhelmed by the surge of bitterness and sorrow that she cried even harder. But after she calmed down, she was able to think clearly during a brief moment of silence. She knew what people had said about the root of his problem. What Ah-ye had said about two coins making a noise was not entirely groundless. In the past, she had rarely taken the initiative in bed, but he had never let her down when she felt the urge, even when she was having her period. That made her feel better about his irascible attitude. And yet she was peeved about what the other women were saying. *It's so embarrassing!* She heaved a long sigh that frightened Ah-le. He broke the ice as he stared listlessly ahead: "Wang-zai and the others want to divide up the family property."

That comment put her in a different frame of mind; she tensed up and inched closer to him. "Your oldest and second-oldest brothers?"

"They were just here."

"What did they say?"

"I don't care what they say. We'll do whatever they want."

"Did you say yes to them?"

"Of course. Don't be afraid."

She was nervous but happy. "Why would I be afraid? I'm just not sure your mother will agree." She picked up the bowl again and brought it up to his lips. He looked down, and when she tipped the bowl, he reached up to hold its rim. She was pleased, comforted to hear him slurping and swallowing the tonic one mouthful after another. "What a shame that some was spilled."

"Ah—" He grimaced. "What kind of medicine is this?"

"An old gentleman from Taipei put it together for us." She saw that there were a few drops left. "Come on, finish it up."

"What was an old gentleman from Taipei doing in our village?"

"Sightseeing. The wife of the owner of the herbal shop introduced him. He is well known in Taipei." She pushed the bowl up to him again. "Drink it up."

He gave the bowl a reluctant look; there wasn't really anything left. "How much did it cost?"

"Five—five hundred for three days' dosage."

"Five hundred?" he cried out, taking the bowl mechanically and raising his head to drain every drop. He swallowed and scolded her, "Aren't you the spendthrift. Five hundred means nothing to you!" He might have sounded cruel in his complaint about the money she'd spent on his illness, but in her ears it sounded like a compliment.

Imagining what effects the three dosages of tonic at a cost of five hundred might have on his body, he couldn't help but ponder a more practical question: What if she'd been duped? He did not want to think about that possibility, and yet he couldn't stop returning to that question. As for her, she usually recovered quickly from upsetting incidents and rarely showed outward signs of elation over happy events. Having sifted out the praise from his multi-layered reproach, she savored the joy in silence. For a while they were able to put aside the matter of dividing up the family property.

In a small farming village like Guiliao-zai, people divided up family property every year, but that was the first time a Limp Dick problem was the cause. It had been only four years since the family property was divided over the onset of his illness. Ah-le and his brothers were known for embodying the notion that "only blood brothers can be trusted when it comes to killing a tiger or capturing a thief." Hence, Ah-le's health problem exacted a serious toll on the clan coffers; otherwise, the fraternal relationships would not have deteriorated in four years to the point that his brothers were crying foul. To be sure, dividing up the family property alone was not enough for Ah-le to earn his nickname and become a part of village lore. The key was the resounding defeat he later suffered during a fight with Gimpy Ah-song, which, along with his prolonged illness, made the nickname stick.

Why the fight with Ah-song? On the one hand, it had been so long ago, nearly two decades, that even the two men could not remember all the details. Besides, Ah-le's health issues had affected his memory, while Ah-song had drowned after falling into an irrigation ditch a few years back. So no one really knew. On the other hand, the fight had provided such entertainment for the villagers that none of them really cared why the men had fought. Most recalled that it started when Ah-le and Ah-song grabbed the front of each other's shirt.

"Why did you grab my shirt?" Ah-le demanded.

"I wouldn't have if you hadn't grabbed *mine* first," Ah-song replied, somewhat timorously because of his limp.

"Don't ruin my shirt."

"Don't *you* ruin *my* shirt!"

The onlookers burst out laughing. More people gathered to watch, but they made sure to give the men enough space to move about.

"I said don't ruin my shirt," said Ah-le.

"And I said don't ruin *my* shirt," Ah-song replied, feeling more relaxed now, egged on by the gawkers' laughter.

Ah-le looked closely at his opponent's shirt. "What's that smelly rag you're wearing?"

"Same as yours." Ah-song changed his tune when he noticed that Ah-le was better dressed. "What's that stinky fancy shirt *you're* wearing?" Ah-song was pleased with himself for coming up with a retort on the spur of the moment.

"My stinky fancy shirt isn't as ragged as yours."

"My ragged shirt isn't as stinky as yours." Ah-song was beside himself with joy when he discovered that he was witty and clever.

Caught in a stalemate, Ah-le had to seem above the fray, because he had one leg more than his opponent; unfortunately for him, the crowd of merriment seekers made it clear that whoever looked the sternest would lose his audience. Instinctively he knew he was at a disadvantage and wanted to leave as soon as possible without losing too much face.

"Let go."

"You let go," Ah-song mimicked, having won laughter from the gawkers earlier with that trick.

"I'll let go if you will."

"I'll let go if you will."

Disgusted, Ah-le loosened his grip on the other man's shirt as a test, but Ah-song did not sense either the change or Ah-le's weariness. Instead, the laughter egged him on even more, as if he would sacrifice another leg for a real battle. He had wanted to move his numbing fingers, but by accident he tightened his grip on Ah-le, who was then prompted to return the favor.

"You mean it?" Ah-le sounded angry.

"So what if I do?" Ah-song was now emboldened.

"Let go of me."

"You first."

"I'm going to break that other leg of yours if you tear my shirt."

"If you tear my shirt, I'll—I'll—"

"You'll what?" Ah-le retorted. "A gimpy guy like you ought to know where you belong."

"Ha—," Ah-song cried out. "So you're laughing at me for having a limp, but what about you? You're a Limp Dick. Heh-heh—." Ah-song looked around him. "Limp Dick!" He raised his free hand and closed his spread-out fingers to make a deflated gesture, like a wilting lotus flower.

Ah-le was confused amid the laugher, vaguely aware that Ah-song was not his only enemy at the moment. He hadn't done anything to anyone in the crowd, which included people he'd known since childhood. He was on good terms with them, but now they were standing there bursting with laughter as Ah-song spewed his nonsense. They seemed to be on Ah-song's side, not his. Ah-song knew that he had hit his opponent's sore spot and Ah-le was about to lose.

"Limp Dick." Ah-song repeated his hand gesture.

"So what if I'm a Limp Dick? Why are you worried about it?"

"I'm not worried about it."

"Then let go of me." It seemed like an opportunity to turn things around.

"Why should I?" Ah-song tried to move his good leg, but he

had been putting all his weight on it for too long, and he stumbled. As he began to teeter, he grabbed Ah-le's shirt. He was afraid his opponent might misinterpret that as an attack.

"Don't you dare tear my shirt," Ah-le warned.

"So what if I do?" Ah-song was relieved when his opponent reacted with words, not fists.

"Don't you dare tear my shirt," Ah-le repeated, still loud, but not as forceful.

The gawkers were getting bored, so one of them shouted, "A lousy show drags on forever. Get on with your fight or go home and fight the cow in your pen." That brought a laugh.

Ah-le thought that he would have little trouble defeating the skinny, gimpy Ah-song, despite his frail health. But it wouldn't be much of a victory to beat a man with a bad leg; he might come off looking like a bully. Well, go home and fight the cow, then. Why not? He shoved Ah-song's hand away. Ah-song, who had been standing on one leg the whole time, was using his hand on Ah-le's chest for balance. He fell to the ground with a thud once Ah-le shook his hand off. Dazed, they stared at each other until the crowd's laughter woke them up. Ah-song had been enjoying the upper hand, with the support of the crowd's laughter. As he fell, his body weight shifted to the buttock on the side that was less fleshy due to the limp, so skin and bone hit the hard ground; it hurt so much he nearly peed his pants, not to mention the embarrassment of the inelegant fall. Furious, he tried to get to his feet. "I fuck your mother!" he screamed. "Fuck your mother! You asked for it!" He turned over and, on all fours, stared backward at Ah-le. Glaring with bulging angry eyes, he struggled to his feet. "Don't run if you want to be fucked. I fuck your mother; I fuck the thirteen generations of your ancestors!" He finally managed to stand, but with his back to Ah-le, so he had to turn around to confront his enemy from five steps away.

Seeing Ah-song turn around, Ah-le assumed a fighting stance, waiting to defend himself with as little force as possible. He had never been someone to mess with, for everyone knew he had been a favorite student of Master Wuren. When the Xipi and Fulu gangs got into a fight, Ah-le had helped the Fulu win. Ah-song knew all about the other man's victories, and the fall was a painful reminder of Ah-le's martial arts background. But the pain and shame made him wave his arms with clenched fists like the chained balls in the hands of Luo Tong, the hero of a Tang novel.

"I fuck your mother!" he hobbled at Ah-le. "You can't get away with bullying a gimpy man."

In reaction to Ah-song's crazed approach, Ah-le crouched down and wrenched his back. He nearly cried out in pain, owing to his weak kidneys, and lost his balance. Before he had time to think about what might happen next, Ah-song's balled fists landed on his head, then all over, until he curled up and felt the blows on his buttocks. Ah-song had never expected Ah-le to be beaten so easily; his fists must have been more powerful than he knew. "Gimpy Ah-song is no pushover!"

Dizzy from the pain in his lower back, Ah-le was happy to be on his hands and knees, which spared his tender spots and let his buttocks take the brunt of the attack. He regained his composure, finally sensing how ridiculous he looked. *No one would say I was taking advantage of a gimpy man if I gave Ah-song a good beating now, would they?* he said to himself. His determination to beat Ah-song intensified when he heard the jeers from a crowd that was clearly having a good time at his expense. But he had to put himself on the offensive first. "Stop!" he shouted. "Stop now, or I'll show you what I'm capable of."

Ah-song realized he might have gone too far, but he couldn't stop simply because of the shout. Besides, his fists had a mind of their own, and ever since the moment he'd decided to fight, they had moved like an automated machine; he couldn't have stopped now even if he'd wanted to. The same went for his mouth; he cursed almost as a musical accompaniment to his hands. "I fuck your mother! Fuck your mother!"

Ah-le couldn't hold back any longer. Fixing his gaze on the other man's leg at his eye level, he wrapped his arms around it to give himself a boost. "I fuck the stinky cunt!" That curse opened the floodgates, and he couldn't stop, either. Caught by surprise, Ah-song fell backward and landed on the ground with another thud. He righted himself angrily and quickly threw himself at Ah-le. As they wrestled on the ground, Ah-le felt another stab in his lower back. He let out a scream, then curled up to moan in agony.

Ah-song got to his feet and looked at him; he put his hands on his hips not thinking the other man was seriously injured. "Do you still want to fuck my mother? Come on, I'll take you there."

Some of the onlookers walked up to check on Ah-le.

"Are you all right, Ah-le?" Jinchi squatted down to check him out.

"My back." Ah-le pointed at his lower back. "I hurt my back."

Jinchi tried to help him up, but Ah-le waved him off, in obvious pain. "Don't touch me. Let me lie here for a while and I'll feel back better. Tell them to back off."

Jinchi stood up and said to Ah-song with a smile, "That was impressive, Gimpy Ah-song."

"Want a screw? Let's go, then," Ah-song said smugly. "I'll take you to the brothel in town—my treat."

"Let's see if you've got the money first, Ah-song," someone jeered.

He took out several small bills. "Here's the money." He paused to think. "Have I forgotten anything? I could bring a woman here and have her strip naked, and you, Limp Dick Ah-le, wouldn't be able to screw her. And you were saying you wanted to fuck my mother?" He cast a superior look at Ah-le, who was still on the ground.

"You'd better get out of here, Ah-song," someone shouted amid the laughter. "Ah-le's oldest son is here."

While everyone was looking in the direction of the temple entrance, Ah-song turned and limped off, muttering to himself.

After his friends had helped him home, Ah-le slumped over a lounging chair, looking dazed, while his wife pulled off his clothes, as if looking for lice, and asked him where he'd been hit and where it hurt. He remained silent except to sigh when he was reminded of the painful events in his life, his eyes open wide, looking like a mackerel at a fish stall oblivious to the bustling shoppers.

He sat up in bed. After draping a blanket over his lower body, his wife left him alone to brood. She didn't know what to do with him. The food she'd brought to him in bed was getting cold; she tried her best to console him, but he was unmoved. That went on until ten at night, when she came in to take the food back to the kitchen. She had been hungry, but the food held no appeal when she looked at the untouched dishes and the husband who had turned a blind eye to his dinner. After washing up and smoothing down her clothes, she went to the sacrificial table in the main room, where she lit an oil lantern. The flame, the size of a chicken heart and with a black tail from the smoke of the kerosene, jumped intermittently, casting an eerie, flickering, shadowy glow on the pictures of deities: the Red Boy, Third Prince Nezha, Mazu and her attendants All-Hearing Ears and All-Seeing Eyes, as well as the Earth and Kitchen Gods. Lighting the three sticks of incense in her hands from the flame of the lamp, she touched up her hair and smoothed her clothes one more time before she stood in front of the table and, holding the incense by her chest, intoned softly with her head tilted slightly to look at the deities,

Bodhisattva,
Prince Nezha,
Kitchen God,
Benevolent Earth God. In the past,
On your holy birthdays, New Year's, and other holidays, the head of the house, Huang Dingle, always prepared sacrificial offerings to pay his respects. He is a loyal follower of yours.
And he is well regarded in the Guiliao-zai area.
He had a fight with Gimpy Ah-song this evening, and if he's suffered any internal injuries,
Please make sure he's safe and sound.
And please make sure he eats something.

She bowed deeply, inserted the incense sticks in the burner, and held her palms together to show her reverence.

"Are you still up, Mother?" their third son called out when he passed the room on his way to the toilet.

"Come over here to pay your respects to the deities and ask them to take care of your Ah-pa." She handed him three sticks of incense. "Here. Ask them to protect him."

Displaying nothing to indicate either objection or consent, the boy did as he was told.

"Go on, tell the deities." She stood next to him. "This is Huang Ah-chang, third son of the head of the household, Huang Dingle," she said when he remained silent. "He is here to plead for your protection of his father. He's a filial son—"

The boy put the incense in the burner before she was finished.

"How's Ah-pa doing?"

"Don't go in there now. He doesn't respond to anything, like a block of wood."

"What happened to him?"

"Go to sleep. We'll talk about it tomorrow."

After making her obeisances at the table again, she took the three burned-out sticks out to the kitchen and laid them in a washbasin before pouring in all the remaining hot water from a vacuum bottle. She took the hot water to their bedroom along with a towel, which she wrung out, folded, and tested the temperature on the back of her hand before placing it over Ah-le's face. "I hope it's not too hot." He continued to ignore her. The towel did not feel hot to her, so she used it to wipe his face. "Why are you acting like a block of wood? I've asked you so many times my tongue is about to fall off, but you still won't say a word. Even a mute knows how to grunt." Grumbling good-naturedly, she wiped his hands and feet and had him sit against the side of the bed.

"Time to sleep. It's almost midnight. What's the use of getting angry? You'll get sick holding everything in like that."

Startled by her husband's prolonged silence, she got out of bed and looked sideways at him. His eyes were still open, and he was breathing evenly, his chest rising and falling. She touched his palms and found them warm.

"Go to sleep and stop scaring me. I have to get some sleep even if you don't want to." She lay down and pulled up the blanket, but she wasn't sleepy. Her eyes were open, too; she felt his incessant sighs thumping against her heart. At some point she began sighing along with him.

On such a quiet night, everything resurfaced in the minds of those who could not sleep. Ah-le thought back to the street fight between the Xipi and Fulu factions years earlier. They were in the courtyard at Guan Gong's Temple. He had one foot on Boar Linzai; with one hand he grabbed and twisted the hand of Dabi, the bodyguard at the Laikuai Brothel, and with the other he nimbly caught the club in Lushan's hand and used it to beat the famed Erwang Lushan to the ground. After that, Ah-le-zai, Master Wuren's top disciple, helped the Fulu Gang quell the Xipi Gang, which had been terrorizing the temple for years, and retake their territory. For a while he was installed in the seat of honor, facing the chicken head at temple celebrations. Naturally, he was revered in Guiliao-zai, where many of the youngsters took pride in his victory. He was asked repeatedly to mediate arguments between village men, and no one defied his rulings. Another sigh escaped as he recalled his glorious past.

His thoughts went to the shops in the village. The owners had always said something like, "Come on in, Ah-le-zai," when he walked by. "What would you like?" Even if he didn't want anything, the courteous greeting made him stop to window-shop. "Nothing. I don't have any money on me, but I'll be back another time."

The shop owner would smile broadly. "Hey, we're not strangers. We can't let money come between us. That's so un-neighborly."

Unable to refuse the invitation, he would go in and pick out something small, since he really didn't need anything. He would pay cash if he had the money and put it on credit if he didn't. But not long before, when he had wanted to put a can of fish on credit at Ah-tou's shop, the man showed reluctance. As for his sons, they stopped offering him cigarettes unless he asked for one. But the more Ah-le thought about it, the more he realized that he had been wrong to blame the changes on others, for he was the one who had changed. Strangest of all, he wasn't upset with people who no longer showed him respect; nor did he harbor a grudge against Ah-song. He did not view his sons as misbehaving or unfilial when they did not give him spending money without his asking for it. *I'm the one who has become worthless; I can't even work in the field. I'm the one to blame—I am.* These thoughts made him sigh throughout the night.

The resounding defeat at Ah-song's hands must have helped Ah-le see himself more clearly. And there was something of equal importance in terms of his physical strength and willpower—that was the role of a man of repute like him in Guiliao-zai's small circles, in others' minds, in a family with relatively strict moral and ethical codes, and in the production structure of an agricultural society. After a long night of rumination and self-reevaluation, he realized, to his great surprise, that the Huang Dingle he used to know was gone. The discovery sent a chill through his heart; the pain in his lower back became unbearable. His face was so twisted from the pain that tears rolled down his cheeks. It was more than he could take, and he began to wail. It was an emotional release that his body needed; it made him feel good and led to even louder wails, like the buffalo that had howled before dying from a serious injury two years earlier.

"What's wrong?" His wife, who had been awake all night, bolted upright, turned, and shook his shoulder. "Tell me," she said in a choked voice, "what's wrong. Come on, tell me. Please."

But no matter how much she shook him, he continued to wail in that scary way. She began to cry when nothing she did helped, though in the end she managed to calm down enough to try to figure out what was happening to him.

"Where does it hurt? Or are you upset about something? Tell me, please. What—what am I supposed to do when you act like this?"

She got out of bed and groped her way over to the five-watt hanging light bulb. By then Ah-le's face was streaked with tears; a small snot bubble quivered above his lips.

His late-night wailing not only woke the family, but even neighbors whose houses were several plots of land away rushed over to see what was wrong. Soon their bedroom, the hallway, and the main room were filled with curious and concerned neighbors; those closer to Ah-le offered a few comforting words, while those farther off talked among themselves in small groups.

"Ah-le-zai, Ah-le-zai," his gray-haired *shugong*, his grandfather's younger brother, called out to him. "That's enough, Ah-le-zai. Really. Whatever is bothering you, you need to talk about it to feel better. Don't hold it in like that or you'll die from the unhappiness."

"It's late, Le-zai. Even Shugong came to console you, so listen to him." Ah-le's wife turned to Shugong when Ah-le remained unmoved. "You see, he's been acting like this, no matter what anyone says. Please, Le-zai, don't be like that."

Initially Ah-le was feeling so wronged that the outburst brought him relief, so he didn't care about anything else, be it waking up people or drawing the neighbors to watch. But as he continued, his wail seemed incongruous with his need to console himself, and he began to sense that all these people might turn what had happened into a laughing matter. He couldn't let that happen. So when he heard his wife plead with him, he broke his evening-long silence and shouted loudly: "I want to die. I don't want to live anymore. Let me die." He unleashed a broken string of cries interspersed with his loud wails, rocking back and forth on the bed. Oddly enough, he was embarrassed by the impulsive shout that he wanted to die, and yet he seemed to have expelled the blockage inside that had caused such pain. Rather than be ashamed of his action, the more he shouted, the more natural it felt; now the onlookers were feeling sorry for him. His wife was sobbing, and others were on the verge of tears. The shouts seemed to draw a new supply of tears out of his body, which was clearly caused by the sympathetic crowd.

"Let me die, then. I should be the one to die." His wife put her arms around him to stop him from rocking. "Please stop. What did I do to deserve this? I suffered when I was young; now I'm old and you're acting like this."

"That's enough, Ah-le-zai. Stop it. What are you trying to do?" Shugong took Ah-le's hands and gave them a violent shake, as if trying to wake him from a terrifying dream. "Ah-le-zai. Open your eyes and look at me, Ah-le-zai. I'm your *shugong*."

"No, no. I want to die. I—I—waah—" All the wounds in his heart became visceral now, with his wife's tender arms around him and his *shugong*'s kind hands holding his. He wanted to be comforted. And for some reason, sensing how pitiable and weak he was made him want to act like a child. So he drew up his feet and kicked out with another shout. "I want to die. I—" He twisted his back again. "Ai-yo! My dear mama, my back, my back, my …" His voice faded until no more sound came out, despite his moving lips.

"See, you wouldn't listen, and now you've wrenched your back again." His wife stopped crying to help Ah-le, who had gone rigid, immobilized by the pain. "You're a man in your forties, but you're acting like a child."

"Let him lie down," Shugong said.

"I'll help him." A neighbor, Qingfan, walked up.

"Wait!" Ah-le's wife stopped him. "I know what to do when he hurts like this. He has to lie down slowly on his own."

Soon Ah-le was moaning. Gently pushing his wife away, he gestured for everyone to leave the room. They went out to talk in the yard, but their conversation was interrupted by Ah-le's moans and cries from the bedroom.

"Something else must be wrong. He couldn't be in this much anguish just from losing a fight with Ah-song," Shugong said.

"He usually seems fine."

"There has to be something else on his mind, or he must have suffered an injustice to act like that. I know him well; I watched him grow up. He was like an iron man, and I've never seen him cry." Shugong continued, "You have to know that the only time a grown man wails like this is when he's truly heartbroken."

"Yes!"

"It's a good thing he cried. He might kill himself if he didn't."

"The deities have been watching over us," said Ah-le's wife, looking mildly pleased. "He was like a block of wood when he came back after the fight. He sighed until close to midnight. I kept an eye on him, afraid he might try something stupid. But the more I thought about it, the more frightened I got, so I burned incense to ask for the deities' help. See what happened? He began to wail before the incense sticks had burned all the way down."

"That's it," Shugong said. "That's it."

"The deities are truly omnipotent," she said to her children. "Come on, boys, let's burn some more incense to them."

"Ai-yo! Hanxiao—," Ah-le called out amid his moans.

"Ah-pa is calling for you, Mother."

"You burn the incense, and I'll go see your Ah-pa." She raced into the bedroom.

She soon came back out and headed toward the kitchen.

"What happened?" Shugong asked.

"The pain made him wet his pants," she whispered with a laugh. Everyone else laughed, too.

After a transforming night of torment, he returned to the familiar surroundings of Guiliao-zai as his usual self, except that he was stuck with the embarrassing nickname "Limp Dick Le-zai," which everyone considered fitting. Many things felt new and strange to him, including the look in people's eyes, the weight of a carrying pole or a hoe, and his recollections of his past. Compromise is essential to anyone who wants to survive, including Huang Dingle. To be sure, there were many ways to concede. Take his problem, for example; it never got better, and he no longer had any excuse to resent people. But the realization alone was not enough to help him through life, because he needed someone else to blame beyond himself. The degree of his pain and diminished abilities did lessen, but that was as a result of a different way of looking at things, not because he was able to let go; either that or he got used to the new situation or became numb to reality. In his view, the way his wife exhausted herself to cure his problem could be analyzed from two perspectives—she was doing it for him or for his problem. If it was really for his problem, she was doing it at least partially for herself, if not entirely. In fact, Ah-le heard that when men gossiped about him and his wife, they often said that she ran around looking for help for her husband's problem because she didn't want to be a grass widow. Granted, some spoke up on her behalf when the men were reluctant to praise her wifely virtues.

"Stop saying she doesn't want to be a grass widow. She may be hot to trot, but who can say if she truly cares about her husband or if she simply refuses to be a grass widow."

Ah-le heard only the first half when the gossip reached him, but that's all he needed to hear. He could continue in this permanent sorry state as long as she didn't know about the two related ways he was looking at the situation. In his mind he went back and forth between them. When the agony over his impotence was so extreme he wanted to die, he would lay that on his wife, which helped alleviate the pain in his heart. As time went on, however, he felt the pain less frequently. On the other hand, he reproached himself and the affliction when he saw her running around trying to find a cure. It all depended on his mood, and he chose whichever was best for his health. He had done a remarkable job from the outset in choosing between the two, so he never despaired, though he was usually unhappy.

For her part, his wife accepted her lot in life; she would be a grass widow, then, after two fortune-tellers told her that it was her fate. She gritted her teeth, sometimes clenching them hard, which slowly became a habit that was well known in the village. No one seemed to know why, though, and she could not recall when it had begun. Once she was aware of it, it got worse whenever she tried to stop doing it. More than a decade later, her oval face had turned square and her cheeks were visibly more muscular, like someone who has been chewing betel nuts for years. It gave her a determined look.

A long time passed. Ah-le no longer felt any pain when he walked around the village with his nickname, while the villagers treated it as just another name. When someone ran into him on the path as he was returning from town, his back slightly bent, he might be greeted with "Just coming back from town, Limp Dick Ah-le?"

"Yes, that's right. Is your daughter-in-law improving after the snakebite?" he would inquire politely.

"Yes, she is. It was a water snake, so it wasn't serious."

And so it went. It was surely a misfortune that Huang Dingle suffered from impotence for more than two decades, but it must be considered a minor contribution to the small farming village of Guiliao-zai. Besides giving the village its own vivid all-purpose adjective, his medical history served as the old folks' most potent argument against having sex with a menstruating woman or a woman who was still in the lying-in period. It was also a powerful warning tool for women to use in stopping overzealous husbands who wanted to have sex during those times. The educational function of Ah-le's experience also ensured that his four married sons would give their wives' bellies at least two months off before trying for another baby. The young couples in the neighborhood kept Ah-le's affliction in mind and never acted rashly in the heat of the moment.

1974

Mr. Presently

The Three Deities Temple in Wenzikeng—Mosquito Hollow—was small and in no way grand, a perfect fit for this hillside village. Weatherworn, it was a good match for the run-down farmhouses, old cats and dogs, and aging folks left behind. A gloomy but peaceful aura shrouded the place all year round, lending it a leisurely, comfortable ambience.

The temple was pretty much the village's cultural center. Hardly a day passed when children did not come there to while away the time, spraying the place with happy laughter and sad tears under the shade of the banyan tree on sweltering days and in the side room in the cold of winter. And there wasn't a day that old-timers did not gather there to relive their bitter past and mull over their pride in enduring hardships.

Someone was coming up the stone steps leading to the temple; his silvery hair turned into a flash of light by the three o'clock autumn sun shining down on the group.

"Presently is here," a man facing the steps looked up and said.

The others either turned their heads or shifted their positions to glance toward the steps, and then coolly resumed their positions. The man sitting in Presently's spot moved over to make room on the bench for him.

"I had one too many at lunch and overslept," he said as he brushed off the bench with the newspaper in his hand.

"You're lucky you can sleep. I can't. My eyes stay as wide open and bright as the brass rings on a door till midnight every night. I can even hear an ant fart."

"I'm like you. The strange thing is, I'm not sleepy when I first sit down, but pretty soon I'm nodding off, and I keep doing it until I fall out of the chair."

"It's the same for all of us, so what's the point in talking about it? We're old, that's all."

There were thirteen of them, each sharing his experience of getting old and drawing agreement from the others.

"Good. Has anyone else brought a newspaper?" Presently smoothed out the old newspaper on his thighs. "We should all bring some back with us whenever we go into town. This is the last one from the pile Jinmao's grandson gave me."

There were several newspapers with large circulations up and down the island, but none delivered to this mountain village. Fortunately these old-timers weren't picky; they didn't mind that the papers were out of date. They had two main sources: wrappings from items bought in the lowland general stores and discarded papers picked up at the train station by someone who had gone into town.

Like rural old men everywhere, they had gathered for years

to talk about things, domestic and foreign, modern and ancient. But they had a daily routine that was not shared in many other places, which was for Presently to read the papers to them. No one had asked or forced him to do so, nor was he promised any monetary gain. Afflicted by a severe asthmatic heart condition as a middle-aged man, he had required plenty of rest, so to kill time, he had decided to read the papers for his elders. He never expected that he'd still be doing that as a seventy-five-year-old man. Now he read to his dwindling number of old friends. It had been going on for so long that he felt strange when he didn't do it, and the others felt out of sorts if they didn't hear him read. In the process they formed tight-knit relationships, even though on the surface things might have looked quite casual to others. His nickname was solidly rooted in the small mountain village, overshadowing his real name, in which no one was interested. Most likely hardly anyone knew it, and few wanted to, anyway. The nickname replaced his real name the first day he read the papers for someone else.

As an elementary school janitor during the Japanese occupation and the only villager who knew how to read, he was tense when he first started reading, so he began with "presently" to ease into the task. A habit quickly formed, and "presently" always preceded his reading; without it he would not know how to go on. He even used the word as a transition to begin a new item or paragraph. He had to translate Mandarin Chinese into Taiwanese as he read, which was not easy; his mind would sometimes malfunction. Unwilling to stop, he would keep repeating "presently" like a broken record until he found the right expression in Taiwanese or an accurate rendition. He would be in a similar state when he did not know how to read a word or did not understand a term.

"Presently" replaced his real name; both were names for the same person, but each represented a different kind of vitality.

"Say, Presently, Mianbei Song's son asked Fuzhou-zai's son to swear an oath by lopping off a chicken's head. What's going on with them now?"

"How would I know, since none of you have given me any newspapers?" Presently removed the reading glasses he had just put on and stared at them.

"I heard they beheaded a chicken at the Temple of the City God."

"Nothing happened. The election was long over."

"Let's get serious. You can swear any oath you want, but you can't behead a chicken just because you feel like it." Afraid that his friend might overlook the severity of the action, Ah-cao, the oldest, was emphatic. "I've seen it myself, back when I was a kid. A woman in Xiazhuang tried to poison her mother-in-law. She wouldn't own up to it even when they showed her the evidence. So the mother-in-law knelt on the ground with her head down and burned incense, demanding that the truth be found by beheading a chicken. The daughter-in-law stuck to her story, but she died the day after the chicken lost its head. Her eyes were gone, plucked out by a chicken, and her body was covered with scratch marks made by chicken claws. The strangest thing was, it had only been a day, but maggots were already crawling in and out of her eye sockets and over the scratch marks."

The sun was still visible in the sky, but the occasional breeze chilled them as they sat in the dense shade of the tree by the old temple. Arthritic joints tingled and ached. The men held their breath as Jinmao murmured, "What happened to the chicken after they chopped off its head, Ah-cao?"

"Now you're asking for it—" said Kunshan, the man with the loudest voice. A burst of laughter swallowed up the last half of what he said, so no one heard it. Radiant sunlight slanted in through the leaves to warm them again, seemingly melting their tongues to smooth out their talk.

"But you have to agree that beheading a chicken no longer works. That's why the candidates so casually ask their opponents to do it. I'd do it if they asked me to."

"Do you know why it presently no longer works?" Presently rolled up the newspaper and used it as a baton.

"Do you?" Zhan Ah-fa asked.

Presently stared at Zhan. "Are you testing me? There's a reason I'm called Presently." He could barely contain his elation. He had discovered the reason after racking his brains the night before, and on his way over to the temple he'd been dying for a chance to show off. Now was his chance. "In my view, beheading a chicken doesn't work anymore because they're all American chickens, caged laying hens raised on feed, no matter how many are used. Presently, whoever dares chop off the head of a local chicken—" He had more to say, but he had to stop to take a breath before he could finish. "Pres—present—presently, that would be fun to watch." Pressing his right hand tightly against the left side of his chest, he felt an abnormal heartbeat, which reminded him that he must stay calm.

"Hmm, that makes sense."

"Then, then—" Jinmao couldn't hold back, but Kunshan cut him off before he could finish.

"You're wondering about those chickens again, don't you?"

"Yes! Then—"

His words were swallowed up by another round of raucous

laughter. Some of the men had tears in their eyes; others were busy wiping the corners of their mouths.

The only one not laughing was Jinmao, who felt picked on. What was so funny about wanting to know what they did with the chickens? He had no interest in eating them; he was just puzzled by the whereabouts of the headless chickens. It was easy to imagine the scene of a chicken being held down on the ground, but where did it go afterward? Did someone take it? Was it eaten or discarded, and if so, where? As someone who had suffered hunger as a youngster, he simply could not get past these questions.

"Let me ask you, Jinmao. Presently, when was the last time you ate chicken? Presently, if I put a *chick* before you, what would you do with it?"

They laughed again, for the third time within a few minutes, which tired them out, but also gave them a sense of being rewarded.

"Be a good pal, Jinmao, and let Presently finish, will you?" Ah-fa said.

Jinmao had said nothing because he was unhappy, but now his sense of injustice flared up at the "request" from Ah-fa. He opened his mouth, but Ah-fa cut him off before he could say a word.

"Wait! Wait! Wait a second!" Ah-fa turned to Presently when he saw Jinmao clam up. "Presently, your turn."

"Presently—where was I?"

"Beheading American egg-laying hens."

"Ah, yes. Presently, think about it. Once its head is chopped off, the ghost of the chicken goes down to the underworld to lodge a complaint, but the King of Hell can't understand what the American chicken, raised by big-nose foreigners, is saying.

The chicken can't understand the King of Hell, either, so it can't get his permission to ask for its life back. That's why beheading an American chicken doesn't work. That's one of my theories." Presently stared at Jinmao, fearing he'd say something to make the others laugh again and interrupt his planned speech. Raising his voice, he charged ahead. "The other theory is, presently, these American chickens are all egg-laying hens with white feathers. But you need a rooster to swear an oath, because the ghost of a rooster will be relentless when it's asking for its life back, but, presently, what could these hens do?"

He could tell that most of his friends were dubious about this theory, so he raised his voice even higher: "That's what the newspaper said, the newspaper—" His right hand went up to press against the left side of his chest again when he felt his heart beat out of rhythm.

From his long experience in reading newspapers to old folks, he had learned that his listeners believed him unconditionally when he told them that something came from the papers. So he bolstered the credibility of his views by invoking the authority of a newspaper, which reinforced his tendency to spout his opinions and criticism, though he made sure to sound fair-minded. When arguments arose, he loved to remind others to use reason and logic.

"You have to be logical. Presently, I can give you another example. My daughter-in-law, Wenlong's wife, stewed roosters for their oldest son just before he hit puberty. Not a single whisker grew on the boy after he ate two roosters. Later we realized that caged roosters raised on feed are useless, so he switched to a local breed. Ha, guess what? Presently, his voice broke after eating just one, and he looked like a little adult. Presently, isn't this the best proof? So certainly only a local breed would work, don't you think?"

When Presently used commonsense logic and combined what he'd learned from daily life with what he'd read, plus folk beliefs, whatever he said sounded plausible to his circle of temple friends, especially when he leaned on the authority of newspapers.

"That must mean that beheading a chicken to swear an oath still works."

"Best not to test it, though."

The others joined in, mainly to agree with Presently, which pleased him mightily. Meanwhile, Jinmao had finally managed to say something he'd wanted to say for the longest time, while his friends were too distracted to stop him. "So no one knows, then?" He was still hung up on the beheaded chickens.

Even Presently laughed this time, since he'd had a chance to expound his views.

"What's the matter with Jinmao? Presently, whoever knows what happened to the beheaded chicken needs to tell him right away; otherwise, presently, he'll never give up."

Jinmao totally missed the tongue-in-cheek nature of the comment; he actually felt that Presently had articulated what he had in mind. "Yes, that's right. That's it!" Jinmao looked contented, as if he'd been holding it in for a long time and was finally able to let go just before the dam burst.

A sense of congeniality spread among the circle of friends now that Jinmao was no longer in distress. Presently's natural inclination at a moment like this was to pick up the newspaper and start reading, so he would be the center of attention. Smoothing out the rolled-up newspaper, he put on his reading glasses and cleared his throat.

"Presently," he ahem-ed when he noticed that not everyone was listening. "Presently." He looked down at the paper once he was sure he had everyone's attention. "Presently, Mr. Huang, a resident at Fugu Village. In other words, in a village called Fugu there is a man named Huang, whose cow delivered a calf yesterday that looked like a baby elephant. You hear that? Ah, presently, the guy whose last name is Huang has a cow, and that cow had a calf yesterday. But it didn't look like a calf, it looked like a baby elephant. Quiet, everyone, there's more. Presently, the owner took good care of the calf, but unfortunately it died the next day."

The old folks' curiosity was piqued, even though it was a minor item added to fill a corner space of the newspaper.

"Fugu Village?"

"Is Fugu Village Mosquito Hollow?"

"That's right. Mosquito Hollow is Fugu Village."

"There can't be another Fugu Village, can there?"

"Right. It's here. Presently, I nearly forgot, and it escaped your attention, too."

Even in their wildest dreams, they could never have imagined that a remote place like theirs would be in the paper. It was a minor news item, but a major event for them. They were overwhelmed by the special attention.

"Mosquito Hollow?" Ah-cao the elder said. "Mosquito Hollow? I don't know much about other places, but if it was in Mosquito Hollow, everyone, and not just me, would know about it. When did the news appear?"

Presently froze. He too knew everything about Fugu Village, just like everyone else, and yet he could not recall anything like that taking place. But he had been speaking for and through the newspaper for so long that he had to question his own knowledge.

He looked at the date. "October twenty-first."

"What's today's date?"

No one could answer that right off.

"Today is the third day of the lunar month, so then it should be—"

"It doesn't seem too long ago, because we just had the Double-Tenth Holiday."

"Who cares how long ago or what date is today," Kunshan said. "I haven't stepped out of Mosquito Hollow even once. I would've *had* to know if something like that happened here. Besides, none of you heard about it, either. Don't you think that's strange?"

Wherever he looked, Presently saw puzzled eyes staring back at him.

"Wait. The Zhan family, the one by the temple, is the largest in Mosquito Hollow. Then comes the Zhang family in Pizikou, followed by the Kulianjiao Lins; the rest are families in Kengding. There is no Huang family." Ah-cao stared at Presently. "And cows? We all know there are only three left in the village, two with the Zhan family and one at Kengding. Where did *that* cow come from?"

Presently knew all that, too. He had wanted to add his own questions when the others looked at him suspiciously, but he chose to side with the newspaper, unable to make up his mind. Since he'd started decades before, reading the newspaper to other people had only elevated his social status and reputation in this small mountain village; this was the first time he had been put in such an embarrassing situation. And he misjudged their reaction, thinking that his friends had already taken an adversarial stance, which irritated him, and that made his heart race and his breathing erratic. Sensing another asthma attack coming on, he grabbed the left side of his shirt tightly.

"That's nonsense. A cow in Mosquito Hollow gave birth to an elephant?" Jinmao blurted it out, but no one laughed this time, because he had said what was on their minds.

Presently looked at Jinmao, unhappy that such an ignorant person should be calling him out. He thumped the paper and shouted, "That's what the paper said. Don't you believe it?"

The others, whose doubts had put them on the attack earlier, quietly retreated and only displayed their suspicions on their faces, probably because Presently had raised his voice or because they were reminded of the news source.

Amid the momentary silence, only the sound of a ripped newspaper was audible; the half-sheet that had fallen to the ground from Presently's right hand fluttered in the wind.

Everyone realized that Presently was about to have an asthma attack. They did not feel like arguing over a minor news item, but he would not give up.

"Everyone, presently let's go to Kengding to have a look before the sun sets, and we'll know if a cow gave birth to an elephant."

No one said anything.

"Presently, let's go have a look, since that's what the paper said." He looked around and continued with a weary smile, "That's what the paper said."

The sun was sinking below Kengding. With Presently in the lead, the old men followed the narrow path alongside a grove of acacia trees as they climbed up to Kengding.

The space between them lengthened as the sun got bigger on its way down. The lower it sank, the redder it looked. Now lagging behind the others, Presently was gasping as he wrapped his arms around an acacia tree. He tried to say something when

Jinmao stopped to check on him, but nothing came out. A spasm wrenched his body, his hands released their hold on the tree, and he slowly slumped to the ground, just as Jinmao raced up anxiously. The last thing Presently saw was the towering figure of Jinmao.

Kunshan, who had the loudest voice, was first to reach the top. Gazing at the sun, which had lost most of its radiance, he turned to shout to his friends, "We're here!"

That was met by a response from Jinmao, the one who never joked: "Presently is dead—"

The silence was palpable.

"Presently is dead—"

1986

Blind Ah-mu

It was a windless day, and the air was so icy it could shatter.

"Hey, Houyang, are you really going to the duck shed on a day this cold?"

A cough in the distance was all it had taken to make Blind Ah-mu raise his voice. He wanted Houyang, who was fifty meters away, to hear him, but he also felt strangely cheerful that Houyang was the first person he ran into that day. Tucking the umbrella handle he used as a cane under his arm, he tilted his face up and stood at the roadside with a smile, waiting for Houyang to ride by on his bicycle.

"I'll be damned if anyone could believe you're blind." Houyang was peeved as he said to himself, *Damn it, I didn't know who it was, but he knew it was me and that I was going to the duck shed to gamble.* Houyang was impressed, but his admiration for the blind man's uncanny hearing gave way to a complaint as he drew closer.

With his head angled toward Houyang, Ah-mu followed the man's movements and silently accepted his bantering curse. Despite the lasting friendship between the two men, Houyang was startled by the whites of Ah-mu's moist eyes when the angle of the dim morning light made them seem to bulge and grow bigger. The unexpected fright made him so unhappy he felt like cursing the blind man again.

And yet Ah-mu seemed magnanimous even when his friend was short and abrupt with him. Turning Houyang's outburst around, Ah-mu sifted out the unspoken compliment in the comment, which brought a smile to his face. From where he was, he couldn't really "see" his friend leave, but he was able to pinpoint the exact direction Houyang was taking. He waited until the man's bike had glided over the hill before touching his cane to the ground and gently tapping his way toward the rear of the village.

Another bike rode his way when he reached the spot where Houyang had coughed. Ah-mu stopped to listen. The rider was in a hurry and straining, seemingly unable to catch his breath. Ah-mu laughed silently when he detected the sounds of labored breathing and the bike's noisy sprocket.

"Qingchi-zai, Houyang just went down the hill—"

"Who cares about him? I'm looking for Xiuying! What do you say to that?" Qingchi said with an edge to his voice. He was not happy that people knew he was going gambling at the duck shed.

This time Ah-mu did not laugh, and he felt the previous moment's cheerfulness vanish. He turned toward Qingchi's receding back and froze. Dizziness overtook him as he recalled his urgent shouts for Xiuying. "You all have eyes, but have none of you seen my daughter?" Ah-mu had spat the words at the village head when he finally managed to swallow the lump in his throat.

"Uncle Ah-mu, I've sent people to ask around."

"After all this time, that's all you're doing, asking around?"

"She's not a child. She can't be lost," the village head said. There was hidden meaning in his comment.

Ah-mu rolled his big, bulging eyes toward the electric light, with only the whites showing. It had been more than a week, but each reminder sent tears rolling forcefully down his face to the corners of his mouth.

No one else said a word. The village head pressed a cigarette into Ah-mu's hand, and he took it. Everyone in the village knew that Ah-mu would not permit anyone to light his cigarette for him; he had insisted on doing it himself since the time years earlier when a prankster had handed him a firecracker. He took out a match, held it between his thumb and index finger, and struck it. When it was lit, he used his middle finger to locate the flame before bringing the cigarette up to his lips with his left hand and moving the match closer. The middle finger on his right hand had a callus from years of feeling for the flame. The curious children in the village loved to play with that finger.

Ah-mu took a long drag and exhaled. "If she's lost or dead, that's her fate. But, but—" He simply could not accept the logical answer that was staring him in the face. Yet it had gotten to the point where he had to bow to reality, even though he still tried to deceive himself; he thought that if he asked the same question often enough, he might come up with an answer that would make him feel better. Adopting a different tone as a hint to the people around him, he hoped to hear someone blame the survey team on his behalf.

"Has everyone in the survey team left?"

"Yes, they left last week," the village head said with a glance at the people around him.

"That's strange! What are the chances that they took off with my sweet little girl?"

"I don't mean to criticize you, Blind Ah-mu," the village head's father cut in, "but I'm from an older generation even though I'm not much older than you, and that gives me the right to say something. You won't find another girl in our village as well behaved as Xiuying. You don't appreciate how lucky you are. No matter what she did, you shouldn't have hit her with your cane just because she came home a little late a few nights. Have you forgotten how old she is? You have? Well, I'll tell you, then. She's in her thirties, and should have been married long ago. At the very least you should find a man willing to marry into your family. Have you thought about that?"

"All right, Ah-pa, that's enough," the village head said.

"No, you're right. Keep going, Brother Rongkun. Don't stop." Ah-mu had regained his composure and pleaded with those around him: "Everyone, please tell Xiuying when you see her that I want her to come home. She can hit me back if she wants to. That's true, I mean it. I mean what I'm saying to you today. I—I want her to hit me back, as long as she'll come home."

Ah-mu was glued to the spot, lost in thought, as he turned in the direction of the road going downhill.

"Why are you standing here on a cold day like this, Ah-mu?" It was Uncle Xianglei taking his cow out to graze, but Ah-mu had failed to notice until the man greeted him.

"Ah, yes," Ah-mu answered in a startled voice. "You're out early."

"It's so cold. Go home and put on a winter coat." Xianglei stressed the last three words, as he noticed the tattered army jacket the blind man was wearing.

"Yes, yes, of course." Ah-mu's heart ached. The other man might as well have been talking about Xiuying when he mentioned a winter coat. Ah-mu wouldn't have to worry about it if she were around. Earlier that summer, their house had gone up in flames and they'd lost everything. Xiuying was busy getting people to rebuild the house while gradually replenishing other supplies until their life was as comfortable as before. He hadn't expected her to run away with someone soon after winter arrived, not long after she'd said she would take him into town to buy some clothes.

Now that Xianglei's comment about the weather had reminded him of his daughter, he felt the bone-chilling cold spread across his back. He shivered while counting the layers he had on. "A vest, two sheets of newspaper, two short-sleeved undershirts, one long-sleeved shirt, and an army jacket. Wow, seven layers. No! It can't be seven layers or I'd be wearing a shroud. The newspaper should only count as one, so six in all." Feeling better with the new tally, he turned his head to listen carefully. Not far away the cow was snorting, so Ah-mu shouted, "Lei-gong! Several layers of summer clothes count as one winter coat, don't you think?" He paused. "Lei-gong!"

Xianglei didn't respond, but Ah-mu believed that the man was laughing.

Ah-mu was buoyed, sensing that he'd discovered a new logic. He tapped his cane rhythmically to create a relaxed beat.

The sun was not up yet, but the farmers were when he reached the rear of the village. As he walked along, he chatted with the villagers who greeted him. With the older ones or those from his generation, he could call out their names with ease. It was harder with youngsters who weren't from Dingzhuang.

"Ah-mu. You're up early."

"I sure am. What vegetables are you offering today?"

"Green onions and garlic. Want to take some home?"

"Thank you, but I'm not going home yet. Will you get a good price at the market?"

"No, not at all." The man, Jincai, pulled the cart uphill as he added, "Drop by the house and get some."

"Anyone helping you with the cart?" Ah-mu said from the roadside.

"Yes." Jincai pulled with his head down. "Today's Sunday, so my two little grandsons came along to help."

Ah-mu had more to say even after the cart had passed. "Those two grandsons of yours are wonderful kids."

The two boys, who were pushing from behind, looked at each other with a happy smile before pushing even harder to help their grandpa's cart up the hill.

Ah-mu was about to walk on when someone else came up. "Where are you going, Uncle Ah-mu?" It was Huixiong, pedaling hard to get up the hill on a bicycle carrying turnips.

"Jincai's grandsons are really good kids, aren't they? They came to help their grandpa with the cart." Ah-mu paused and changed his tone. "Ai-yo! The uphill road is really steep. Who are you?"

The young man had been going full speed up the hill, but he lost his momentum when he approached Ah-mu. He jumped off to right the bike before it toppled over. "My grandpa is Degen. I'm Huixiong, his youngest grandson."

"Oh, Degen is lucky to have a youngest grandson as old as you."

"My grandpa's at home with nothing to do, so please go see him when you're free."

"I will, I will," Ah-mu said. "What are you carrying? It seems heavy. Want me to help you push?"

"No, thank you." The offer seemed to make the young man

nervous. He pushed hard. "I'll be off now. It's still early. You should stay in bed longer on such a cold morning."

The mention of cold gave Ah-mu a sense of complacence, though somewhat prematurely. He thought it was the perfect moment to use the same reasoning that had convinced Lei-gong a while ago—"Several layers of summer clothes count as one winter coat." But it seemed a bit out of place, so he swallowed the words, no longer feeling so complacent. He wasn't done talking, though, and when he heard Huixiong going up the hill, his eagerness to say more gave him a brilliant idea. He turned and shouted, "Hey, eh—" He'd forgotten the young man's name. "You, Degen's grandson. It is cold, but walking around outside is better than wearing ten layers of clothing, don't you think?"

Ah-mu's reply came too late for the exchange to make much sense, and to Huixiong it sounded more like an axiom picked up on the road. He wanted to stop and think about it, but the uphill climb would not allow a loaded bike to pause, so he kept his head down and pushed the turnips to the top.

Everyone in Baishilun had made an effort not to mention Xiuying in front of Ah-mu. Because of the unspoken agreement, his mood had lightened even though it had been only a couple of months since his daughter left. But on this day, Qingchi's earlier insolence and his friends' diligent children brought back a memory of his daughter:

"I know you're a hard worker, Xiuying, but I don't know what to say when people tell me you're a pretty girl. Is that true?"

"Don't pay attention to nonsense like that."

"It must be true. Why else would people keep telling me that?"

Xiuying was quiet.

"Wouldn't it be wonderful if I could see your face?"

It was a few days after that conversation that she hadn't come home.

A deep longing had replaced his bitter resentment, and the sorrow he usually felt was nearly gone. The new discovery, along with his response to Huixiong, lifted his mood again.

As he walked on, he tried to hold on to that shred of happiness while reproaching himself for being heartless. *Why else would I no longer feel the same intense pain when I think about Xiuying?* He berated himself: *Why am I like this? It hasn't been long since she ran away, but I'm not sad anymore. Why? What am I happy about?* Yet he could not suppress his happiness; all he could do was smile helplessly at his inability to be depressed.

Ah-mu was well known in the village, even to an old mutt like Heizui, which could not be bothered to yap at a stranger. But he barked each time Ah-mu walked onto Jiuru's threshing floor.

"What have I ever done to you, Heizui? Get lost."

"Don't send him away. Have him come over and get a taste of my cane."

When the dog heard Grannie Jiu's comment, he lay down by the doorsill after a symbolic, ineffectual bark. The spot was still warm after he had spent the night there, and now the warmth heated up his belly as well as the fleas.

"I was just going to get Ah-quan to take this to you," Grannie Jiu said. "Come on in. It's so cold out there."

"Next time. It's getting late," he said from beyond the eaves.

With a brazier in one hand and the other pressed against the wall, she replied in a tiny but shrill voice that resembled the clanging of thin metal sheets, "Well, based on the date and time of Xiuying's birth, it would be better to do it between three and five in the afternoon. Too bad you can't find any of her clothes, but the hairbrush will do. When you get home, leave a bowl of water outside the door, hold the brush, and call out three times, 'Come back, Xiuying.' Then put the hairbrush on her bed, and wait three days before you take it off. Got it?"

"And that will do the trick?"

"Yes, it will. Wait." She called into the house. "Are you ready, Ah-quan? Uncle Ah-mu is waiting for you."

"It's too early to wake him. I'll go get it myself."

"He gets up early to read, so don't worry. He listens to his grandma. It's easier for him to carry the water bowl."

"Let's go." Ah-quan bounded out and picked up the basket by its plastic handles. Inside were a bowl of rice with a paper figurine stuck in the middle, two bowls of simple food, and a hairbrush.

"Don't forget to call out three times." The metallic voice followed them out the door.

As they walked out of the village and reached the hill, Ah-mu felt a skylight open on his forehead. Instinctively he knew that the sun was up. He stopped, tucked the umbrella handle under his arm, brought his palms together, and stood for a moment of silence, facing a morning sun that had barely risen above the ground.

Ah-quan turned and saw Ah-mu framed in a red glow. He was so touched by the mood of the moment that he didn't move until Ah-mu walked up to him.

"Uncle Ah-mu," Ah-quan whispered, "do people worship the sun?"

"I don't know, but I'm not worshiping the sun. I'm paying my respects to light." He continued, "I was born blind, did you know that?" He refrained from giving a further explanation. "Are you still holding the basket?"

"Yes." Though Ah-quan was curious about the blind man's respect for light, he did not pursue the matter, but not out of a fear of anything. They were simply under the spell of something mysterious, especially Ah-quan, who was quietly soaking up the ambience.

"Ah-quan." Ah-mu sensed something different about the boy, but Ah-quan didn't hear him.

"Ah-quan!"

"I'm right beside you, Uncle Ah-mu."

"I know you are. Let me ask you something. Does becoming a surveyor require a lot of schooling?"

"Sure it does. Some members of the team that came to do land adjustment in Zhongpu graduated from college before they took the surveyor exam. Mr. Dai, the head of the team, and several others are engineers, while the others—"

"What year are you in?" Ah-mu couldn't wait for him to finish.

"I'm a senior in high school."

"Do you want to become a surveyor?"

"That's beyond my reach. We're talking about engineering, and that requires a test score of four hundred to get in."

"Four hundred?" Ah-mu had no idea what four hundred meant for the college entrance exam, except that it sounded pretty high judging by Ah-quan's tone of voice, so he made sure to express his astonishment.

Ah-mu suddenly had a favorable impression of the survey team. He heard someone ask, "Where's your daughter, Xiuying?"

"Oh, she left with the survey team to become a surveyor," he replied with a happy smile.

Ah-quan was amazed that Ah-mu could be so bluntly forthcoming about his daughter. He looked at the blind man, whose bulging eyes were rolling, only the whites showing. He made a mental note to tell the girls in his class what he'd seen that morning.

"Uncle Ah-mu, some of my classmates who live in town said they want to come see you," Ah-quan said excitedly.

"To see me?" Ah-mu responded. "What's there to see?"

"They want to see you light your cigarette and look at your middle finger—"

"What else did you tell them?"

"I—"

"Did you tell them about finding the matches?"

"Yes, I did."

They both laughed, Ah-mu so hard there were tears in his eyes.

Ah-mu had been in the village head's house one afternoon looking for matches on the red lacquered table where they kept incense sticks and candles. He groped around and eventually knocked something over. "Oh, no." He quickly righted the bottle and brought his wet hand up to his nose. "Perfume," he said. "Must be Ah-qin's." What a waste, he thought. So he rubbed the liquid on his face, then scraped the table to get more and spread it over his neck and shoulders. Everyone, young and old, doubled over laughing when he walked out of the house.

"What's so funny?"

"It's not time to offer thanksgiving to the temple, Ah-mu, but you're prepared to get on the stage," Qingtian said.

"Shut up, Qingtian."

The gawkers did not want Ah-mu to know right away what he had done, but then it dawned on him. *Get on the stage?* he said to himself. *Ah, the clown. Could I have knocked over a bottle of fountain pen ink? Yes, that's the smell of ink.*

He decided to put himself out there for everyone's merriment. But then he spoke up boldly. "I don't laugh at you, so why are you laughing at me? I can't see, so it's perfume to me even though it's ink to you. So what?"

They had not outsmarted him. He was quite pleased with himself, even as he tried to imagine what he must look like. So he laughed, nonchalantly, along with the others.

"Were you there?" he asked Ah-quan.

"No, but the story has spread."

"What other humiliating stories about me have you told your friends?" Ah-mu asked with a smile. "Did you tell them about me feeding the pigs?"

"Yes. By the way, where are the pigs now?"

"I had to sell them before I could kill them." He no longer found it funny when he thought about the two young pigs, which had weighed between forty and fifty kilos each.

The task of feeding the pigs had fallen to Ah-mu after Xiuying's unannounced departure. Clever and spry as dogs, they would stand up on their hind legs to intercept the swill before it hit the trough, spilling the mixture of yam leaves cooked with food scraps. Ah-mu quickly learned to keep a club in his right hand and hold the bucket in the left when he fed them. He cursed and waved the club to chase them off as he poured the swill. But they were too smart for him; they would split up, one drawing him away with the club while the other sneaked up on him. The swill would still splash all over the pen. Worse yet, one time they nudged the empty bucket into a corner of the pen, forcing Ah-mu to go in to retrieve it. They knocked him down as soon as he was inside, standing on mushy yam leaves. The club fell from his hand and landed somewhere he couldn't see. When he tried to stand up, he slipped again and fell heavily on his backside; he cried out in surprise, only to frighten the pigs, sending them charging around the pen. Feeling utterly helpless, he sat there and began to cry. "It's all right if you want to stay away, Xiuying, but you have to be at my side when I die. I'm going to die now, Xiuying."

Dusk descended, turning the dim pigpen even darker. Alerted by his wail, the neighbors came to check on him.

"Oh, no. Which one is the blind man?" someone cried out in alarm.

The bitter experience from a few days earlier had taken on an intoxicating flavor from rumination as he looked back. Ah-mu's mood lifted when he heard the delighted boy's unstoppable laughter. Like Ah-quan, Blind Ah-mu felt sorry for and yet amused by pig-feeding Ah-mu.

Ah-quan was reluctant to leave when they reached the chinaberry tree in Ah-mu's yard. "I'm putting the basket here, Uncle Ah-mu. I'll be off now." He took Ah-mu's hand and touched it against the basket.

"Good, that's good. Leave it here. You're such a nice boy. Thank you very much."

After Ah-quan left, Ah-mu crouched down to recall the instructions from the boy's grandmother. Mentally following the metallic voice, he had placed the bowl of rice with the figurine and the vegetable bowls on one side when he heard someone ask out of nowhere, "Where's your daughter?"

"Are you still here, Ah-quan?" Ah-mu was startled.

But no answer came. The boy was gone, already on his way down the hill.

"Ah-quan!" he called out again, his voice now anxious.

Silence.

Now he remembered. Back on the hill, he had thought he heard Ah-quan ask about his daughter, but it wasn't the boy. *No wonder Ah-quan talked about something else when I told him Xiuying had joined the survey team,* he said to himself. With his head raised slightly, he sat motionless on his haunches, waiting to hear the voice again. His eyes rolled this way and that as he tried to focus, but the imaginary voice was elusive, like a fragrant orchid in a room, undetectable when you try to capture its aroma yet redolent when you ignore it.

Urged on by the need to finish between three and five, Ah-mu went into action. Cradling Xiuying's hairbrush in his arms, he called out, "Come back, Xiuying. Come back, Xiuying." This was the first time he had called his daughter in such an affectionate way. He had never imagined that calling her name would cause him so much pain and yet move him so much. When it came to the last time, he wanted his voice to be loud and emotional, but his throat tightened up. In the end, he sounded bleak, his voice trembling in the icy air, when he called out one final time, "Come—back—Xiu—ying!"

1986

Swatting Flies

August's sunshine isn't that much different from July's: equally prickly on the skin and harsh on the eyes long before noon. Flies and humans take shelter in the same shade; sometimes the humans swat the flies not for health or sanitation reasons but simply out of boredom.

Old Mr. Lin Wangcong was sitting on the porch, his back against the door. Flyswatter in hand, he had been smacking flies since morning, when the ditch across the alley was still shaded by his house, and was still at it now that the shade had receded to the front of the house. As the temperature rose, the number of flies grew; the more he swatted, the more they came, with no end in sight. It was tedious, and wouldn't do any good no matter how long he persevered, a thought he'd had since he'd begun smacking them after moving here in the third lunar month. But to Old Mr. Lin, who was hooked on the activity, the thought was more like a tiny thorn in his skin: he couldn't pick it off, and it was annoying when he touched or thought about it; but it was safe to leave it in. After a while, he discovered that he was a crack shot when it came to swatting flies; moreover, the dead flies were in pristine shape, which demonstrated the perfection of his skill and the right use of force. As a result, swatting flies now brought him pleasure and had turned into an enjoyable way to kill time. When someone asked why he was swatting flies, he said, "Because they're there." Then he equivocated: "It's like cracking watermelon seeds. You can't stop until you finish every one on the plate."

"But you've got quite a lot already," a young man visiting Lin's neighbor said when he saw the mound of dead flies, looking like fermented black beans.

"The fishermen are in luck today; there are lots of fish."

"How do you know?"

"See all those flies?" Lin followed that by smacking his flyswatter on the ground. He turned it around to show two dead flies, clearly intended to impress the stranger. The admiration on the young man's smiling face elevated this irresistible habit to the level of entertainment.

But the exercise began to lose its appeal when the youngster was called away for lunch. What else was there for him to do? At least this was better than the tedium induced by idleness. He turned to look inside, but detected no movement. His wife would not be up until one or two in the afternoon, he was sure. It must have been three or four in the morning when she came home. He thought he had heard a rooster crow, but his memory was hazy, as he'd been in a drunken stupor after downing a whole bottle of rice liquor. All he recalled was Ah-fen banging on the door angrily. "I know you're doing this on purpose," she screamed. "I'll show you what I'm capable of tomorrow if you don't open the door this minute."

He felt like he was dreaming.

"Damn you, Cong-zai. Did you die in there?" The banging was

getting urgent, followed by mumbles. "I can't believe you could be so mean." She raised her voice again. "Damn you, Cong-zai. Do you want me to die of anger?" More banging.

The racket slowly became real to Wangcong, who, still in bed, heard some neighborhood dogs barking at the commotion. Rattled, he tried to get out of bed, but for some reason he seemed weighted down and was unable to move. The more frozen he became, the higher his anxiety rose.

"Lin Wangcong, now I see what a vile, vicious man you are." Ah-fen was getting hoarse.

He was sweating, knowing he should not make her wait or wake up the neighbors, whom he would have to see at daybreak. Since he could not get up at the moment, he thought he could at least respond to her call. But when he opened his mouth, no sound came out. He took a step back in his thoughts.

He thought he must be dreaming.

Ah-fen continued to curse and bang on the door.

He doubted that he would know he was dreaming in the middle of a dream. So he tried to get up, or shout a reply, but could neither sit up nor make a sound. That was evidence enough that he was still dreaming.

"With someone like you, the earlier you die, the better. Do it now, and I'll be reborn." She was getting hysterical.

He heard her every word, so he didn't think he was dreaming. *Could there really be such a strange dream?* he asked himself. *Could someone be this clear-headed in a nightmare?* The thought sent him into a frantic effort to wake up, as he feared he'd die of suffocation otherwise. He willed his body into action and his mouth open, his mind struggling at the same time. As he lay in the dark bedroom, he began to panic.

Then everything went silent.

It stayed that way for quite some time.

The silence did not soothe his mind; on the contrary, he was tenser than ever. Strangely, the weight that had immobilized him earlier vanished just as he strained but failed to hear Ah-fen's voice. He sat up and touched the space beside him. It was empty, and he was confused again. His head felt heavy, though the cobwebs were slowly clearing. Sitting there dazed, he felt dampness on his forehead; a cold shudder racked his body.

"Damn. What a terrible dream," he muttered as Ah-fen began to wail outside as if she'd been walloped by a sad thought.

"Ah-cong—Ah-cong. Don't die, Ah-cong. I'll die with you if you do, Ah-ah-cong." She turned to direct her plea to the neighbors. "Ah-yong, Tu-sha, be good boys and come help me break down the door. My Ah-cong is dead."

The dogs were barking even more fiercely now.

Now Wangcong was fully convinced that he was tangled up in a bad dream. In his mind's eye, he saw himself leap off the bed and run down the stairs barefoot, shouting, "Fen-zai, I'm alive! I'm not dead, Fen-zai!"

As the door opened, he saw his tearful wife, framed by half a dozen neighbors in their PJs.

Ah-fen, who had been filled with worry and racked by sorrow, was reassured when she saw him and immediately changed her tone. "You're not dead?" she screamed. "Why are you still here? Are you staying alive just to get on my nerves?" She slapped him.

Still feeling the effects of the alcohol, Wangcong had been wavering between his dream world and reality, but the slap ended any confusion.

"Are you crazy?" He had to fight back in front of all these

people.

"Who's crazy?" Ah-fen shot back.

The couple's exchange dispelled the neighbors' worries; they were all too tickled to say anything. The older ones knew it was a prelude to an imminent reconciliation.

"You shouldn't be out gambling," the old man cried out unhappily when his apology was rewarded with her tirade.

"What would I—I do if I didn't go gambling? Tell me. What should I do?" She stammered, aware that she was in the wrong.

"I—"

"What about you?" She cut him off. "Ever since we moved here, you swat flies during the day and go drinking at night. Is that all you can do?"

"What—what do you want me to do?" With reason on his side, he should have been able to talk back to her confidently, but he had unwittingly fallen into her trap, and she had put him on the defensive with her accusation.

The old couple had only each other, but they could never express their true feelings or show that they cared about one another. Sometimes when trivial matters arose, they blurted out the exact opposite of how they really felt and ended up upsetting their spouse. Ah-fen had slapped him because she was embarrassed that he'd heard her sorrowful words about him; but such incidents occurred often in their daily life, and he had no trouble dealing with them.

His wife was still asleep, so he kept swatting flies. He had pretty much lost interest in food since moving out of Neipizai five months before, away from their land, leaving him with no more farm work. On the other hand, he had a greater appetite for alcohol, though with significantly less capacity for it. Ah-fen would not have had so many reasons to nag if he hadn't been hospitalized several days earlier after taking a drunken fall and cracking his head.

No sooner had a fly landed than the swatter came down; the fly was dead faster than it knew what hit it. The whole process took so little time it had no one to blame. A month after swatting like this, he had developed a new technique, though he didn't kill all the flies this way. It depended on the situation and his mood, as well as his ability to fix his gaze on a fly when it was circling before landing. Which was why it did not happen often. Whenever he felt like employing his new technique, he chased the fly off the ground and waited for the right moment. Flies have a habit of coming back to land on the same spot after being waved away; it would scratch its head and flick its wings, which felt like a taunt to anyone the fly had harassed. Old Mr. Lin's new technique ensured instant death. Wanting to use it this time, he focused on a fly that was about to land in front of him, making it possible to forget to complain about Ah-fen not getting up to make lunch.

Yet the appeal of fly swatting paled in comparison to the stubborn hold that reality had on him. The first of the month had come and gone, and he grew tense whenever he heard a sound like the mailman's motorcycle, especially around noon, the usual time for mail delivery. He had yet to see the mail carrier on this day, and though he would not admit it, he very much hoped to see him. Back in the third lunar month, his eldest son, Lin Bingyan, had fallen to his knees and begged his father to resolve his debt by giving him the deeds for the land and the house. To keep Bingyan out of jail, Mr. Lin had done what he asked, though he did not understand what his son meant by a favorable turn after the emergency passed. The son had promised to send six thousand

NT via registered mail on the first of every month to cover the old couple's expenses, but he was often late. They'd have been in serious trouble if not for their three daughters, who helped out with a thousand or two every now and then.

"I'm well into my seventies," Wangcong sometimes grumbled, "and I've been called just about everything—grandpa, granduncle, great-grand-uncle, and more. I've been a lot of things to a lot of people, except cuckold, of course. In order to socialize with people, I have to deal with all sorts of occasions: when someone has a new baby, or moves into a new house, or has a son going into the army, or is getting married, or is being hospitalized, or announces a funeral. Do you know how much I need to spend each month?" It sounded like he was reading off a list, but anyone who heard his rhythmic litany would both be amused and feel sorry for him; and yet he would say anything to defend Bingyan when people criticized him for mistreating his father.

Another motorcycle flew past the alley entrance. He looked back in disappointment, but the fly had flown away. If he had not held out hope that it was the mailman's motorcycle, the noise would have interrupted his fly-swatting effort; conversely, the movement of a fly would have interfered with his focus on listening for the hoped-for mailman's vehicle. He lost interest in the flies as noontime neared. Straining to hear as much as possible, he eyed the alley entrance, hoping to detect the distant sound of a motorcycle.

It was already the sixth of August. He was concerned about the imminent opening of "Hell's Gate" in two days, the first of the seventh lunar month. They needed to offer a sacrifice to the ghosts. Then on the third day, there would be a village ghost festival, when he would need to feed friends and family members coming to the festivities. He was muttering as his flyswatter landed heavily on the concrete surface. He got one, but it was pulped, and a piece of the plastic swatter had broken off and flown into the street. Several capons rushed up to fight over it. One ran off with it in its beak but dropped it after only a few steps. Bringing the flyswatter up to check the damage, Wangcong reproached himself for using too much force, then struck out again and, with a crisp and light but powerful flick of his wrist, killed a fly that had landed to feast on the pulpy one. Stirring the fly gently with the swatter, he pushed its body over to the wall, where two columns of ants were carrying dead flies away. The more they moved, the more flies that showed up. Capons roaming the area looking for food spotted them and rushed over for their share, but the old man raised his flyswatter and yelled, sending them back a few steps before turning to stare at the flies. Since Ah-fen was not going to get up and make lunch, he thought he would go in and warm up some leftovers. Still hungering for the flies, the capons walked up to a spot just out of reach, cocked their heads, and glared at the old man.

"Hey—damn you! You've got guts, I'll say that for you. Now stay where you are." He stood up. He'd been sitting so long that his back was stiff; nothing worked except the hand holding the flyswatter. With his hands on his knees, he leaned forward and pushed down until he was able to stand. Then, with one hand on the door, he reached behind him with the other and thumped his lower back with his fist. Little by little, he straightened up. But he forgot why he'd wanted to get to his feet once he managed to do it. He finally remembered when he spotted the capons. Taking long strides, he was going up to chase them away when he heard a motorcycle coming his way. It sounded like the mailman's; he perked up and walked to the alley entrance. The capons ran ahead of him, obviously thinking that the old man was still intent upon chasing them off.

The engine sound came closer and closer, but all he heard was his racing heart as he reached into his pants pocket for his seal to sign for the registered letter. The sound got closer until it neared the intersection, where it turned off, likely going in the direction of the Three Deities Temple. The hand gripping the seal in his pocket began to hurt as its corners cut into his flesh. He reached the alley entrance and, standing in the middle of the street, looked to one side and then the other. Someone riding over on a bicycle from the temple greeted him before he knew who it was.

"Have you eaten yet, Uncle Wangcong-zai?" It was Xishui-zai.

"Oh, it's you. Where are you going?"

"To the county office to get the vet. For some reason, our pig hasn't been eating the past two days." He stopped in front of the old man.

"Aren't you going to slaughter it for the festival on the third?"

"Yes. So why did it have to pick this time to stop eating? I'm worried sick."

"How big is it now?"

"Over six hundred jin, but it's lost weight over the past couple of days."

"It's too hot. Like us, it's lost its appetite."

"But but I keep the fan on and give it a cold shower twice a day."

"What do you feed it?" Wangcong was distracted by his concern for his friend's pig, no longer thinking about his own urgent matter.

"Rice balls and watermelons. No worse than what we eat."

"Has any evil spirit been disturbed in the pigpen?"

"It can't be. It's been a long time since we hammered a nail or removed one in there. What spirit could we have disturbed? We don't even allow anyone in mourning or a pregnant woman to get near it."

"Have you offered your respects to the Earth God?"

"Of course! And not only the Earth God. We also prayed to the Three Deities."

"Hmm." Wangcong was pensive. "That's strange."

"I wouldn't be worried if we weren't hosting the festival this year." Xishui-zai pushed the bike along. "Well, I must go get the vet."

"That pig is so lucky," Wangcong mocked himself as he watched Xishui-zai ride off in a hurry. "Luckier than me."

He was about to head back inside when a policeman walked out of a small shop and called out to him. "Mr. Lin, Mr. Lin. Is your wife home?"

"What's the matter?"

"She was caught gambling at Li Mansheng's house last night, and has to pay a fine. Is she home?"

"A fine?"

"Yes. There's a fine for gambling."

"What did you say? What would she do if she didn't gamble?"

"She can do anything but gamble. Is she home?"

"How much is the fine?"

"Six hundred."

"Six hundred? Didn't it used to be three fifty?"

"It just went up."

"The most they win or lose is a hundred or two, but you want to fine her six hundred?"

"Come on, I'll go with you."

Old Mr. Lin stood still at the alley entrance, feeling utterly wretched.

"Mr. Lin—"

"I don't know," he fumed. "We don't have any money."

"You must be joking, Mr. Lin." The policeman softened his tone when he noticed that Lin was angry. "How would you be able to live at Lakeview Villa if you didn't have money? How's this? Please ask your wife, Lin Zengfen, to see me at the station."

The policeman walked off, but Lin felt a stabbing pain in his heart, reminded by the comment about money and living at the villa. The houses flanking the alley were all part of Lakeview Villa.

Hmph! What villa! Looking into the endless alley and the rows of buildings that seemed far way, he could not take another step, though the night-blooming cactus that had come with the move beckoned from the wall of the sixth house on the left. With a heavy heart, he entered the alley, as if walking into a trap even though he knew he'd been taken for a fool.

He raised his head to a more comfortable angle and took in the view of the villa. "Damn!" he said contemptuously. "Villa? Hah!" For some time he had been growling like that, often realizing how foolish it was only after he'd done it.

Wangcong knew the area like the back of his hand: there was a date orchard by the Three Deities Temple midway between Dapi and the Neipizai hills, and anyone from Neipizai going into town had to pass through Dapi. Thousands of dates had vanished overnight when the county road was paved, replaced by the sudden appearance of a six-meter-wide alley with thirty-two single-family two-story houses facing each other. Everyone knew they had been finished in a hurry before a building ban went into effect. There was more sand in the concrete, and the shoddy quality of the cement was in plain sight after the stencil plates were removed. The workers who had built the houses said they wouldn't live there even if it were free. The builder's reasoning was simple: people in Dapi and Neipizai didn't need and couldn't afford houses like these.

They were built for urbanites, even people from Taipei. Hence they had a tiled exterior, beige on the second floor and dark brown on the first, plus orange slanting eaves. Every house had a small garden that was two and a half meters wide and eight meters long, and a fence one and a half meters high, with two five-meter-tall Chinese junipers and four azalea bushes. Advertising billboards for "Lakeview Villa" hung on utility poles all the way from the No. 9 Highway to the site. The "Lakeview" in its name was not just hype; there was indeed a small lake there, as well as a potter's field on the hillside two kilometers from the construction site. Thirty-two square meters in total, each unit had four rooms, two baths, and a kitchen. At a million eleven hundred thousand NT, only nine units had been sold since they'd come on the market two years earlier, and that was after a five hundred thousand reduction in price. Currently, a down payment of only three hundred and eighty thousand was required, and still there were no takers six months after the reduction. The final sales price was naturally a disappointment to the developer. Moreover, urbanites and Taipei residents had bought none of the nine units sold; all the owners came from Dapi or Neipizai. The developer was not the only one who was surprised by this; Lin Wangcong and his wife had never imagined they would move into a two-story house in the villa.

"Bingyan is so accomplished he can afford to move you into a villa for a life of ease." He had been heartened by compliments like that, but now, five months later, he realized that he had been too smug too soon. Whenever their friends or former neighbors from the village passed through the area, they would stop by to visit them and bring along some vegetables or fruits. They would say something like: "Bingyan comes back to see you often, so you ought to get him to come see us in Neipizai, too. Or at least you should have us over to have a look at the boy from Neipizai. He has a car now, so he can come and go easily."

He felt trapped by these comments from his friends.

Ah-fen was still in bed. He wanted to get her up, but a fear of his wife stopped him. He could not recall when he had begun to fear her, but it was clearly after their move. She was his second wife. They were twenty years apart in age, but that difference meant nothing; in fact, it made him the envy of all the men in the village. When he stopped working and his body began to show signs of aging, she was in her early fifties, with a hardy, stumpy build and a voice that could be heard from one end of the alley to the other. The fishmonger, who made frequent rounds to their village, loved to compliment her on her figure, so flattering her that she would respond with a smile, ignoring Wangcong, who was with her. "I may be getting old, but my nipples are still as small as the tips of chopsticks. I don't know if it's true, but I've heard people say that women with small nipples are blessed with filial children."

Wangcong would be too ashamed and outraged to stick around when he heard his wife talk about her nipples with another man. Her disgraceful reply made him more diffident than ever, but he lacked the spunk to say anything.

He put a plate of fish on top of the leftover rice in the electric cooker, replaced the lid, and pushed the on button before casting a fearful glance at the top of the stairs, where he thought he saw Ah-fen's shadow flash in the dim light of the landing. Puzzled by that imagined sight, he walked to the doorway and saw that the sunlight had moved closer to the doorsill on his side. The pile of flies by the wall was gone; so were the two columns of ants, all but a few stragglers conducting a disorganized search under the sun. He went out into the alley; the capons were nowhere in sight. The shadow cast by the empty house across the way sent a warm feeling through his heart. He went back inside, opened a bottle of rice liquor, picked up a bowl, grabbed the swatter from the wall, and went across the alley to the vacant house.

The unsold houses in Lakeview Villa were all pretty much the same, with silver grass towering over the juniper and swallowing up the azalea bushes. As he sat on the doorsill of the empty house, he drank and swatted flies; at least he didn't have to worry about the mailman for the rest of the day, since it was long past his arrival time. No motorcycle sound, however similar, could disturb his focus on swatting the flies.

It was getting hotter, and there were more flies than in the morning. Soon a small mound of them attracted worker ants to carry them away. But the more he flicked the swatter, the worse he felt; it no longer felt like killing time. The matters that caused him grief came at him one by one, like the flies. He thought of Ah-fen's gambling habit, her comment about her small nipples with another man, and ... Whenever a fly landed, he smacked down hard and didn't care if it ruined the swatter; he no longer took the time to estimate the right force. One by one, the flies were smashed into pulp and stuck to the ground, and yet they continued to come. He thought of his son, the temple festival on the third, the policeman—and his own powerlessness. He smacked with a vengeance, but the more he swatted, the harder it was to forget all the disheartening matters; they came after him like the flies, and he would never be able swat them away.

A motorcycle roared into the alley.

He kept smacking the flies.

It stopped in front of his house, followed by a shout from the mailman: "Registered mail for Lin Wangcong."

Another fly was turned into pulp. He looked up at the mailman, but felt no elation or anxiety when he heard the shout.

"Registered mail for Lin Wangcong. Don't forget your seal."

He couldn't stand up right away, despite the effort. His heart stirred, out of elation or maybe anxiety, when he heard the mailman shout the second time. He wanted to shout back, but a tightness in his throat stopped him; he had his voice but couldn't use it, for fear of making the wrong move in front of the mailman. Filled with anxiety, he felt his body grow increasingly tense the more he tried to stand up.

Left with no choice, he picked up a pebble and threw it at the mailman when he called out the third time.

The new mailman turned his head and saw him.

"You're Lin Wangcong?"

He nodded and began to tear up.

1986

The Ghost-Eater Is Here

Muddy-Water River

Muddy-Water River
Before I met you
You had already flown from Grandpa's mouth into my ears
Yet many villages
Many pigs and chickens, ducks, cows, and sheep
Many voices crying to heaven, crying for their children, crying for help
Many people and water ghosts
Were all lodged at the bottom of my heart

Muddy-Water River
I crossed you to leave for a faraway place after I grew up
When I think of home, I think of you
Everything that was lodged at the bottom of my heart woke up
Turned into strings of stories
Flowed from my mouth
Into the ears of children born in another place

These stories often make them
Cry out in frightening dreams, or
Smile in happy ones
I know why they cry out in shock
But I have no idea why they smile

The rainy season dragged on forever. The rain not only came down well into the lunar sixth month, but it got heavier when it merged with the common rainfall around the time of the Dragon Boat Festival.

The Taipei-Yilan Highway, which is over fifty kilometers long, comes alive and looks mysterious in the never-ending rain, especially in the mountains. When you emerge from the tunnel and drive through the twists and turns into Yilan, you can see that the road is not laid out passively for motor vehicles to travel back and forth. On the contrary, it feels more like the highway is making all sorts of vehicles follow its bent arms to roll this way and that. Otherwise, you would not see traffic accidents and their injured or dead victims at so many spots each day; signs put up by the Taipei and Yilan county governments banning the scattering of spirit money might have been effective in stopping the practice. The drivers of trucks, gypsy cabs, and cars usually spend at least forty NT on spirit money that they throw out along the way, a toll and an offering to ghosts they cannot see.

With the prolonged rainy season, the coastal artery, originally designed to lessen the traffic on the Taipei-Yilan Highway, suffered a major landslide in the Shuiliandong section, as if to keep up with the mudslides and landslips in central Taiwan. As a result, traffic on the Taipei-Yilan Highway got worse, and there was a record number of accidents, giving rise to more ghost stories. Shops at bridgeheads and in foothills set up special roadside stalls to sell spirit money to drivers passing through.

The drivers threw paper money everywhere along the way, but mostly in the most treacherous sections, at sharp turns, sites of previous accidents, and at roadside shrines for the Earth God and Wish-Granting Ghosts. On a clear day, the paper looked like swarms of yellow butterflies landing on the grassy road shoulder. When a car flew past, the butterflies fluttered into the air, as if startled into flight. Vehicles created whirlwinds, and the spirit money that rose and flitted in the wind looked more vivid, like real yellow butterflies, in the shifting lights. When no cars came by, the butterflies rested on the grass and resumed their original shape as spirit money, quivering and waiting for the arrival of another whirlwind. On rainy days, the paper stuck to the road surface and, as it accumulated, turned into yellow warning signs. No wonder a tourist was so filled with praise when he mistook the sight for a creation by a conceptual artist.

On this rainy day, traffic was lined up behind a diesel truck straining to make it uphill. Most vehicles running on gasoline were powerful enough for the drivers to get out of a traffic jam by ignoring the double yellow lines. But there were too many twists and turns, with cars and trucks constantly tearing down the hill from the opposite direction, so passing the truck was out of the question. Traffic backed up until the line reached the foothills of the next mountain. Complaints and curses were heard inside the stuck vehicles, and many drivers kept their left wheels on the double yellow lines, ready to pass.

One of them was a nine-seat VW van carrying eleven

passengers, all girls except for the driver, Xiaoyang. Two were Americans studying Chinese in Taipei. The other eight were classmates of Xiaoyang's kid sister, Xiaoxiang. Unlike people in the other vehicles, they were in no hurry and inched forward. They did not mind being stuck on the highway, as they talked and laughed, sometimes even screamed. The American girls were more diligent about throwing spirit money than passengers in other vehicles. The group kept an account of the wrecked vehicles along the way; at some point the total reached seven, but someone insisted on eight. Finally they all agreed there were eight, for the number accentuated the eeriness of the Taipei-Yilan Highway and heightened their sense of adventure. They read the signs nailed to trees and utility poles out loud: Buddhist blessings like "Namo Amitābha" or "Namo Ksitigarbha Bodhisattva," and occasionally "God Loves You." Xiaoyang stopped the girls the first time they read the Christian sign. "You don't have to read 'God Loves You,'" he said. "Taoism or Buddhism rules over the old men and good brothers along this road, so you can just keep saying 'Amitābha.'"

"Who are the old men and good brothers?" someone asked.

"Don't ask about them while we're still on this road, or they'll think we're looking for them," Xiaoyang warned. He had been teasing these city girls, who knew nothing but studying and fashion, and managed to frighten them so much they were all on edge. "Who are they? They're ghosts, lonely, wandering ghosts, scary ghosts. Every twisted shell of a wrecked vehicle is their creation. Don't take it lightly. See, the people in front and behind us are all throwing spirit money. Why? To whom? You could tell even if you thought through your navel. Look!" The girls cried out in fear, except for the Americans, who were obliviously throwing paper. "Why are you screaming? I just wanted to get you to look at the Buddhist sign on the utility pole."

Soon they were next to the pole. "Namo Amitābha," the girls said in unison.

With so much to occupy and amuse them, it's no wonder they did not care that they were stuck in traffic. Xiaoyang was a good and eager host, but he was making the trip only because all his passengers were girls, including Bai Shan, Xiaoxiang's friend and the most important visitor. This was the third weekend in a row he had borrowed the same van and taken the same route to the same place, where they would see the same person to hear the same story. It had been difficult for him to get the van from his brother-in-law's company for the third time. His brother-in-law didn't object, but his sister had raised a stink: "Think about it, Xiaoyang. The romance between your brother-in-law and me is ancient history. Back then, you could take advantage of him and have everything you wanted, but I'm a mother of two now, not a pretty young girl anymore. If you keep pestering him like this, he might just decide to divorce me."

"Please don't be like that. Help me out," Xiaoyang persisted.

"You're a busy boy, aren't you? So why are you borrowing a van and going to the countryside all the time?" His sister turned to her husband. "Does the van sit in your company's garage just waiting for him to borrow it?"

Her husband merely smiled.

"This is the last time. All right?"

"You said it was the last time last time, but now you're back—"

"I mean it this time. Don't nag; you're worse than Mom."

"What did you say?" His sister raised her voice.

"Nothing. I'm sorry, all right? Please?"

"Please help him out this time." His other sister, Xiaoxiang, came to his aid. "Bai Shan, the prettiest girl in our department, is going."

"Ah! So you're in love. I thought you said you'd never get married."

"Who says love has to lead to marriage?" Xiaoyang wanted to say, but he decided against it. His sister was always meddling in his love life, so she would consider it a silent yes if he was noncommittal.

"Bai Shan. Not bad," his sister said, thus concluding the loan of the van.

The stop-and-go traffic was a trial for Xiaoyang, an impatient driver who loved to pass other vehicles. His tendency to show off when people were around was exacerbated by the ten girls in the confined space of the van, so much so that he never stopped gesturing, even though he had to keep shifting. It was partly his nature, but he did nott want anyone to feel bored during a silence. When he spotted another sign on a distant tree, he reminded reminded to read it by leading the recitation, "Namo Amitābha," and followed it up with "The Three People's Principle Will Unify China." They were unaware they'd been fooled until they were midway through.

"Don't try that on us. You're terrible," Xiaoxiang reproached him, on everyone's behalf.

"You're so dense. The Taipei-Yilan Highway connects Taipei and Yilan Counties, both headed by members of the Independence Party. They would never allow that Sun Yat-sen slogan in their jurisdictions." He was pleased with his sense of humor, but no one laughed at his joke, and a temporary silence took over. Afraid that the quiet would spoil the mood, Xiaoxiang asked, "How much longer, Xiaoyang?"

"Probably two more hours with a jam like this. But it's all right. The road will widen when we get to Pinglin, and then we can race ahead of the truck. It will be faster after that."

"Some of my friends here, including Bai Shan, have never heard the story 'The Ghost-Eater Is Here,' so why don't you tell them?"

"Yes, tell it." Even those who had heard it clamored for a repeat.

"Be patient. Wait awhile and you can hear it directly from the old man. You'll get a real sense of the story, so just wait, all right?"

"No, we want to hear it now," they demanded.

"I know you won't believe me, but the best and most thrilling place to hear a ghost story is the spot where it occurred. Tourists who visit castles in England want to hear ghost stories that have taken place inside. The same goes for us. In a little while, we'll be in a thatched hut by Muddy-Water River, where we'll sit around a candle to hear a ghost story told by the old man, a relative of water ghosts. Now, *that* will be exciting."

"Really?" someone asked in a fearful tone.

"Really!" he replied.

"Did you say the old man is a relative of water ghosts?"

"That's what I heard, but I don't know who's related to water ghosts and who isn't."

"You're terrible, Xiaoyang. He loves to scare people," Xiaoxiang complained.

"It's your fault for being so easily duped. In fact, you like to be fooled, too, don't you?"

"You're shameless." Xiaoxiang thumped her brother on the shoulder. "Get on with the story."

With all the girls looking expectantly at him, Xiaoyang smiled. His sister could tell he wanted to wait for the old man to tell them.

"Then why don't you tell us how you met this old storyteller?"

one of the girls said.

That sounded like a reasonable request to Xiaoyang, who was impressed by the girl. She was different.

Who was she? He glanced into the rearview mirror. She was partially crowded out of the mirror, and he could not recall her name. A shy-looking girl, she seemed to really want an answer, so he decided to give her one. He thought back to the day and the somewhat surreal encounter.

He had taken a few photography buff friends to Egret Town in Yilan's Erwanwuzai to take pictures of the egrets. When they got there, they learned that the egrets from twenty years ago were long gone, a disappearance that had been reported in the papers. It wasn't just a disappointment to his friends; it also made him look ill informed. He owned a collection of egret photos his father had taken when he was in the second grade. To show he hadn't come to the wrong place, he asked the man tending a nearby temple, "Is this the place called Egret Town?" He made sure his friends heard the question.

"Yes. Who are you looking for?"

"Egrets."

"Egrets?" It had been a long time since anyone had mentioned them. It was nice to hear about them again, but the man wondered why these people had come looking for birds that had been gone for so many years. He laughed.

"Isn't this the time the flocks come back?" Xiaoyang asked.

"Not anymore." The smile was gone from the old man's face, and a note of sorrow crept into his voice. Stepping out of the temple into the front yard, he pointed at a bamboo fence and turned to Xiaoyang and his friends, who had followed him out. "See that bamboo fence? Thousands of returning egrets would land there, turning it so white that from a distance it looked like a white wall. That's why it's called Egret Town." He fell silent. "But not anymore."

"Why?" One of Xiaoyang's friends asked.

"Why indeed." The old man gazed into the distance at the fence. "Why? There are different theories, but no one really knows why, except that it has something to do with ghosts."

"Ghosts?" Xiaoyang blurted out.

"Ai!" The old man sighed. "It's best not to gossip about others' private affairs." He continued to stare at the fence, his eyes turning into slits, and looked lost, as if the young men weren't there. He was standing still, but his brows and the muscles around his mouth kept tightening and relaxing, not mechanically but more as if they were following a mysterious rhythm. Yes, he saw the egrets coming back in large flocks.

"Incredible." Stunned by the old man's facial expression, Xiaoyang and his friends murmured to each other. "Use your 400 film with ASA 1600, full exposure. I'll help you develop the film when we get home. Hurry," Xiaoyang said. With their cameras clicking away, they photographed the old man while checking his reactions, but he was oblivious to their presence.

He saw the bamboo fence turn white again, but it seemed to catch fire when the setting sun shone down with its red-tinted gold rays. He shook his head in amazement, unsettling the young men so much that they held their cameras behind them and feigned indifference. Moments later the cameras were clicking again when they saw the focused look on his face. They were really getting into it.

"Ah! Wah-wah-wah …" With his hands clasped in front of his chest, the old man shouted excitedly, his eyes fixed on the fence.

Xiaoyang and his friends paused to watch him. One of them circled his index finger at his temple, drawing a silent nod from those who saw the gesture.

"Fire!" The old man said to no one in particular, with amazement in his voice. He had seen thousands of egrets soar into the sky under the red glow of the setting sun, as if startled into flight. But then they changed into raging flames. Looking for branches to land on, the egrets were lifted into the sky by air currents, like spirit money that hadn't completely burned up, and then slowly drifted down. It looked like a city wall. The old man shuddered; he looked down at his arms and began to rub them with his hands. "You see, I get goose bumps whenever egrets are mentioned," he said to the young visitors, unaware that just a moment before he'd been looking as if his soul had left him.

"What did you see?" Xiaoyang asked.

"The fence caught fire when the setting sun shone on it, and from a distance it looked like someone was burning a pile of spirit money. But it's all gone now. Gone. Shortly after the egrets disappeared, people walking by the area late at night heard thousands of egrets flapping their wings to take flight as if startled. Sometimes you could even see the bamboo branches bouncing as if the birds had kicked them before they took off flying."

"Why was that?"

"They were egret ghosts," the old man said confidently.

"Can you still see them?"

"Even the ghosts are gone now." Looking dejected, the old man paused before continuing, "There's nothing now."

That seemed to be his favorite expression; a bleak, sad look appeared on his face when he said, "There's nothing now." His doleful sense of loss was contagious; everyone felt it.

***

Xiaoyang was given to exaggeration by nature, so even a brief description of the encounter made the girls jumpy and put their nerves on edge. At a moment like this, even a prankster would be frightened if someone sneezed or something dropped noisily. Luckily the only potential prankster, Xiaoyang, knew better than to play a trick. A few of the girls, who were so into the story that they wanted more, kept pestering him. "What happened next?" His mind quickly worked out an answer, and he continued with a cryptic smile:

"A few co-workers wanted to go along the following weekend, after they learned that we'd be delivering pictures to the old man and Uncle Shihu, the one who told us about the ghost-eater. So we went, thirteen of us in two minivans. We couldn't find the temple, and naturally not the old man, either, when we got to Egret Town. We thought we must have come to the wrong place, so we asked two men working in the field, but neither of them had ever heard of Egret Town. A third man reassured us that we weren't lost, but he told us the temple was on the other side of the road. It was a tiny graveyard with five or six tombs, which we had missed the week before. We thought it was weird when Tuobi spotted the Kodak film case that he had dropped the previous week when he reloaded the 400 black-and-white film. That had been temple grounds, so how did it become a graveyard? Those of us who had been there the week before were getting jittery, and no one dared mention ghosts. Those who were new to the place thought we were playing a trick on them—"

"But didn't you say you took some pictures and were going to give them to the old man?" one of the girls asked, looking quite pale.

"My co-workers asked the same question, so I showed them the pictures to convince them," Xiaoyang said. "Oh, right, Xiaoxiang, get the pictures from my backpack to show your friends."

A few of the girls cried out fearfully, "No, not me!" "I don't want to see them!"

"I'm not going to touch them." Xiaoxiang was scared, too. She lived at the school dorm and her brother lived away from home, so this was the first time she had heard what he was saying.

The van stopped again, giving Xiaoyang a chance to turn around and ask Xiaoxiang to hand him the backpack. "Don't you want to see what the old man looks like?" He shouted the last few words, but his tone quickly turned serious again. "Take a look; nothing will happen. This is actually a rare picture. We took many that day, but none of them came out except this one. It had some shadowy figures on the negative, and I was only able to developed it by using with special processing. Don't you want to see such an unusual picture?"

"No, we don't. Just tell us what he looks like."

"One look is better than hearing about it a hundred times, ladies."

The American girls could not quite understand what they'd been talking about. Ghosts were nothing new to them, and they found them more amusing than frightening. They did want to see the picture. "OK, we'll take a look at it," one of them said in her accented Mandarin. Most of her tones were off, but it helped lessen the hair-raising eeriness that had been building along the way.

Xiaoyang retrieved a manila envelope from the backpack. Some of the girls screamed their refusal, while the American girls repeatedly said it wasn't all that bad. Xiaoyang burst out laughing and gave himself away.

"Liar! Xiaoyang," his sister yelled out, "you nearly gave me a heart attack." She jokingly punched his arm.

"That's because you're so fat."

She couldn't let that one go; she hit him with her fists and wrapped her hands around his neck from behind, pretending to strangle him.

"The cars ahead of us are moving," someone shouted from the back seat.

Xiaoxiang let go when the cars behind them honked. Xiaoyang shifted into gear and started moving, laughing and coughing at the same time. When he saw another Buddhist sign on a tree ahead, he read it aloud, but no one followed suit.

"You're horrible, Xiaoyang. The old man is still alive, so how could you jinx him like that?" Xiaoxiang said about her brother's prank.

"You won't believe me, but I didn't jinx him; it was never my intention to jinx him," he said with a serious face. "He's dead."

"What? What are you saying?"

"I didn't know about it until last Sunday, when we went to show him the photographs. We offered our respects at his house and put the pictures on the sacrificial table for him to see. His family thought they were good pictures of him." He looked sincere for the first time since they had gotten on the road, so serious that it was out of character, which, along with the residual eeriness, made everyone quiet.

A while later, the American girls pulled their heads back inside the van and said cheerfully, "All gone."

"What? No spirit money left?" He was his old self again. "We're not there yet. What are we going to do about the road ahead?" He turned to glance at the two girls, drawing everyone's attention to them in the process and making them feel if they had violated a serious taboo. "The last stretch of the road is the worst, and you don't want to mess with the good brothers. So what should we do?"

He was talking too fast for the American girls, who were beginners in Chinese. So one of them switched to English: "Did we do something wrong?" They shrugged, spread their hands, and nodded at each other.

Knowing it was just another of her brother's jokes, Xiaoxiang did not want them to worry, so she switched to English to make it easier on them. "Nothing. He was just joking." She tried to explain what he said, but folk customs and cultural practices were hard to convey; the girls did not know enough Chinese, and it was hard to translate the concepts into English. But it gave the group of college students a new subject for their English conversation lesson. They asked each other how to say, in Chinese and English, terms such as "lonely" and "wandering ghosts," "the underworld," "spirit money," "good brothers." Everyone offered ideas, and laughter erupted constantly; without meaning to, they left out Xiaoyang, who had to focus on his driving.

It had been a mentally and physically exhausting trip, even for a show-off like him. In addition to dealing with the stop-and-go traffic, he had to take care of Xiaoxiang's friends, keep things lively, and show off his outgoing personality, humor, and quick wit to impress Bai Shan. The rare moment of quiet when they didn't need his attention felt like an unexpected pleasure. He was tired, and his mind was still in overdrive as fragments of the experience from three weeks earlier flashed through it.

After looking at the pictures, the old man's family thought he was going to demand payment and that it would be exorbitantly high. They smiled and praised his photographic talent when they learned that they were gifts.

"These are wonderful pictures. They look just like him, they really do," the old man's son said, meaning, in fact, that the pictures had captured his expressions perfectly. "It was really strange. He'd been sick for over a month and spent most of his time in bed. No one knew why he said he wanted to burn incense and check out the temple that day. We told him to wait until he got better and we'd go with him. We never guessed that he'd leave on his own and run into you that afternoon when we weren't paying attention."

"He appeared to be in good health when we saw him, just the way he looked in the pictures," Xiaoyang said as he thought back to that day. He couldn't tell that the old man had been laid up for over a month.

"But he spent most of his time in bed after he came back, and he passed away six days later. During the last days, he talked about nothing but Egret Town and the birds. Now that I compare it with your side of the story I finally understand what was going on."

The traffic began to move once they managed to pass the truck, but the rain was coming down harder when they reached the county line, the starting point of Yilan's famous twists and turns. It was only five in the afternoon, but it was already getting dark, just like that day three weeks earlier. The girls' conversation had moved well beyond their destination and ghosts, on to the movie *Titanic* and Leonardo DiCaprio. Xiaoyang listened in as they gossiped about the English poetry professor and a girl in their class. No one reacted with enthusiasm when he told them they'd be there soon. One said she needed to pee, while another said she was hungry, but no one asked if they were in Waizaiwai. They had seemingly lost their eagerness to listen to the story about a ghost-eater from an old man in a thatched hut by Muddy-Water River. *They might even have forgotten all about it,* Xiaoyang said to himself. An acute sense of loneliness overcame him, but at least he still felt the draw of his special feeling for the old man, Mr. Shen Shihu. As the van maneuvered down the twisting road, Uncle Shihu, his voice, and water ghosts came to mind:

Like an eye turned red by conjunctivitis, the last quarter moon hung listlessly above the horizon, about the same height as an old camphor tree. Butcher Yan gave it a passing glance when he was about to cross the river and return to Dazhou for some pigs. He thought he heard a girl crying amid the sounds of the rushing river and wind. Tracing the source with his eyes, he saw a shadowy figure crouching by the river about forty steps away. The sight sent fear into his heart: could that be one of the water ghosts, since this was where there were countless stories about them? He turned to walk away, but to his amazement the shadow gave chase, crying and calling him uncle. He was frightened out of his wits, but she sounded so pitiful; he turned to see a sorry figure, a girl about twelve or thirteen years old.

"Please, uncle. Could you carry me across the river? My mother is sick, and I'm bringing her medicine to save her life. It's dark and the water is running so fast. I'm scared to wade across myself."

"Where—where's your family?"

"My father is Zhu Luocheng from Hongjiaopo."

Butcher Yan was not entirely reassured, but he did not want to be seen as not doing the right thing, so he agreed to carry her over, on one condition. He wanted to use the hog rope to bind her to his back. The little girl thanked him repeatedly before lying down on his back so he could tie her to him.

He entered the river. When he got to the point where the water was up to his chest, the medicine packet fell out of the girl's hand. "I dropped the medicine, uncle," she cried out. "Please pick it up for me."

He had seen something fall into the water, but he told himself it was a typical trick by a water ghost. *She'll push me into the water the moment I reach down for the packet.* Ignoring the packet, he trudged on fearfully. The girl on his back kept shouting until she was screeching; she even tried to struggle out of the rope. In the meantime, she alternated between clasping her hands around his neck and pressing herself down to push him into the water. Taking frenzied big strides, he ran to the riverbank, kicking up water like a startled buffalo. The girl stopped struggling when he reached the bank. Seemingly carried by the momentum of his flight, he kept running until he reached his house. He bolted the door behind him, undid the knot in the rope, dipped his shoulder to one side, and gave it a shake. Ker-plunk. A coffin board fell to the floor.

The memory was still fresh in Xiaoyang's mind; they had photographed Mr. Shen Shihu, who was in his seventies, as he related the story with a demonstration of the shoulder dip. He and his friends were puzzled by the fact that both the old man at the temple and Uncle Shihu had paid no attention to the cameras when they were absorbed in telling stories about ghosts. Hence, they looked expressive and lifelike in the photographs, making Xiaoyang and his friends wonder if luck had played a significant role in their taking good pictures, particularly the candid shots, of which the old man at the temple and Old Mr. Shen were the best examples.

Just look at the old man's face. It resembled a deflated ball, shriveled, misshapen, and wrinkled, with no more than four teeth under or above a black hole, crooked as undisciplined soldiers. As the hole opened and closed, visions of Butcher Yan, water ghosts, the floods from earlier times, and floating corpses materialized under a flickering candle and were transformed into dark, shadowy figures swaying eerily on the grassy wall behind the old man.

"Butcher Yan was shocked beyond belief when he saw the coffin board, and he picked up an axe to split it," Old Mr. Shen said. "Then he shoved the pieces into his stove and turned them into ashes, but he was still scared. So he put a handful of the ashes in a bowl, poured in liquor, and drank the mixture.

"Each time he crossed Muddy-Water River after that, he heard the sound of people running in the water the moment he put his foot in. He also heard them shout, 'The ghost-eater is here.' One day the following year, his body was found near Maozailiao, where the river meets the ocean, after he'd been missing for several days. It was covered with crabs."

Xiaoyang could still recall how Mr. Shen had cocked his head when he finished the story, and a bright light had shone in his eyes despite the cataracts. The young men from Taipei were moved beyond words after hearing it; in addition to words like "great" and "awesome," one praised the story, saying the old man was the true embodiment of native soil. The others repeated the description to show their agreement: "Uncle, you're the true embodiment of native soil."

But the old man did not like the expression; it sounded scandalous to him. He thought he'd been nice to these uninvited guests, so why were they saying mean things about him? "Why am I soiled?"

Realizing that the he had misunderstood the expression, Xiaoyang quickly explained, "You've got it wrong, uncle. It's not soiled; it's native soil."

"Oh, native soil. Why didn't you say it more clearly? I thought you said I was soiled. Hmm, native soil."

They laughed. The old man was not entirely convinced it was positive, though. *Why did they say native soil? Is that really a compliment? Or could it mean something else? It sounds positive, but what kind of praise is that anyway?* He decided not to pursue it further.

"We're coming back to hear you tell 'The Ghost-Eater Is Here' next weekend, uncle."

The young men could not stop saying, "The ghost-eater is here."

When the van stopped at a red light before the Lanyang Bridge, Xiaoyang called out happily, "The ghost-eater is here."

The girls seemed to have just been roused from sleep, as someone asked illogically, "Where is he?"

"Up ahead. We'll be close after we cross the bridge and make two right turns," he said.

"I thought we were there already. So it will still be a while, then."

The rain showed no sign of letting up. It was dark out, and the farm families along the river were on edge as the water level continued to rise.

Speak of the devil and he shall appear. Could it be true that speaking of the flood meant the flood would be there? Shen Shihu was puzzled and worried when he saw that the river was about to overflow into the melon field. Three weeks earlier, a sudden downpour had sent several young men across the levee to seek refuge from the rain in his thatched hut. He was beset by regret when he recalled that he had mentioned in passing the earlier days when the Muddy-Water River had flooded villages, as well as the drowned victims and the water ghosts. But he did not think he had done anything wrong. The Muddy-Water River was all he could talk about, other than ask the youngsters what they did for fun in Taipei. What else could he say to them, if not about the flood and water ghosts in the river? They might have talked late into the night if the man from the repair shop had not come to see them about their tire.

Following the riverbank, Mr. Shen walked from one end of the melon field to the other, muttering to himself: *If the rain continues, the melons will lose their sweetness before the river floods the field. Who would want them then? Any more rain and the melons would crack, and I couldn't pay people to take them.*

He jumped with fright when he got into his hut. "Damn you. Why didn't you make a noise?"

"Grandma wants you to go home to eat."

The old man's heart was still racing.

"An adult like you should have known better. I nearly died of fright, and you're laughing like that."

The pimply boy, the son of one of his daughters, had Down syndrome. He kept laughing since he didn't know what he'd done wrong.

"You go on home and tell Grandma to eat without me."

"No. Grandma said I can't come back if you stay here."

"It's go back, not come back, silly boy. Why can't you see the difference?"

While bantering with his grandson, Shihu thought he heard people shouting in the rain from the other side of the levee—"Uncle Shihu!"

"Quiet! Stop laughing so I can hear better."

But the boy continued to giggle.

Shihu walked out of the hut to look toward the levee beneath a dark sky. A crowd stood on the levee; framed by the evening sky, like marionettes in a puppet play.

"Uncle Shihu!"

"Who's calling you, Grandpa?"

Baffled at first, Shihu cried out in shock as a thought occurred to him. "Oh, no! The ghost-eater is here."

The boy found the cry amusing and ran out into the rain to shout at the shadows on the levee, "The ghost-eater is here! The ghost-eater is here!"

The rain was coming down harder now, as if with increased force from the old man upstairs.

1998

A Story of Nine Fingers

Lianhua lived with her granddad in the mountains, where she grew up. She loved being picked up and held, and only he had the time to do that. On the day Lianhua realized that everyone has ten fingers, she discovered to her surprise that her granddad was missing a thumb. That was also when she learned that not only was there a story behind the loss of his thumb, but that each of his nine scarred fingers had a tale of its own. As a girl she loved hearing stories, so he told her the stories of his fingers countless times, ending with the tale of that detached thumb, which had been reborn to a childless old couple.

When Lianhua grew into her teens, young people were migrating from the mountains to the flatlands as if on a slide, leaving behind a shrinking number of old folks. She had not heard any of her granddad's stories for years; like the mountain itself, he had stopped talking. When she was fourteen, an old soldier who spoke with a strange accent entered Lianhua's house through the iron gates and went straight to her room. The first thing she saw was that he was missing a thumb. Not only was she unfazed by the appearance of a stranger in her room, but she laughed and said, "Ha, you're just like my granddad, you've only got nine fingers." That made the old soldier uncomfortable. Lianhua started taking off her clothes as she talked about her granddad. "Wait a minute," the old soldier said. Not knowing what he meant by that, she kept shedding clothes until she was naked and lying on her bed against the wall, still talking about her granddad's thumb. "How did you lose yours?" she asked as she patted the space beside her. Disconcerted, the old soldier sputtered nervously, "Can … can I be your granddad?" As soon as he said that, she scooped up her clothes to cover her naked body.

"Then how could you sleep with me?"

"Yes, of course, we can't do that."

"Will you tell me a story about your fingers?"

"The fingers have many stories to tell."

"Really?" She was delighted. But she added uneasily, "You still have to pay me."

"I will, I will. I'll give it to you right now, but get dressed first."

The old soldier came by often to tell her stories about his fingers. And Lianhua loved him as if he were her granddad. But then he stopped coming, and a long time went by. One day, some representatives of the Veterans' Affairs Council and a few old soldiers came to see Lianhua, bringing the old soldier's last will and testament. She was no longer there; nor had she returned to the mountain. Word had it that she had been sold to another place.

1998

The Last Phoenix

There is a Taiwanese saying that goes: In the ninth month on the ninth day, the wind will blow the hours away. It has a nice rhythm and rhymes well, but it's also a fitting description of the weather. With the arrival of the Double-Ninth Festival comes the vanguard wind from the northeast, heralding the news that winter will soon be here to take over from autumn. Cold winds blowing low on the ground when warm air has yet to rise out of the way pull kites up from one end and push them forward from the other. The kites not only will fly high, but bells strung together with bamboo and rattan strips ring out as they climb into the sky. A large kite makes a deep, sonorous sound, while a smaller one seems shrill; medium-sized kites fall somewhere in the middle, like a chorus.

A three-day kite festival was being held upstream on the Dongshan River. Large characters inscribed on posters said,

"Fight the wind but not each other." Pros came from all over the island with their kites, chasing away the clouds in the deep blue sky to show off their impressive creations. Bells rang all day long, distracting the children until they couldn't sit still to finish their meals.

Members of the Wu family were feeling festive inside their bamboo fence on the south bank. It was their custom to offer sacrifices to their ancestors on the Double-Ninth holiday instead of separately commemorating the anniversary of each individual's death. It was as important a day to them as New Year's. Everyone, including those who were married and lived on their own as well as those who worked in other cities, returned to offer respects to their ancestors. Every year on this day, grandchildren or great-grandchildren who had yet to learn the value of money would come home and be given a red envelope by Grandpa or Great-Grandpa.

The ritual commenced shortly before noon. The main room and kitchen were not big enough to accommodate five tables, so they set up four for the adults, while the children were given a bowl of rice with meat and vegetables and allowed to eat wherever they wanted. Wu Xinyi, Old Mr. Wu, was so pleased to have everyone home that he could not make himself sit down to eat, even at the urging of his sons and daughters-in-law. Instead, he took a large platter filled with chunks of meat from local chickens and chased after the children to fill their bowls with breasts or drumsticks cooked in a light broth.

"This is the best chicken. Grandpa will kill one for you every time if you'll come home more often." He was oblivious to the fact that these children were raised on hamburgers. For them, chicken had to be fried, and they knew only ketchup, mayonnaise, and

Thousand Island dressing on their food. The chicken pieces from Grandpa were dipped in something black that he called sticky soy sauce, which neither sounded nor looked appetizing. The older kids actually ran away when they saw the old man coming after them with the chicken pieces, whereas the younger ones simply called for help from their mothers as Grandpa dropped some into their bowls.

"You silly kids. You don't know how to appreciate good chicken." The urban children had been acting this way for years on each return visit, but the old man continued to be surprised. After managing to give out only a few pieces, he made another round with his platter. The children turned it into a game of hide-and-seek.

"Don't run away, Timothy. And say thank you to Grandpa." Timothy looked unhappy when his mother stopped him.

The old man was pleased that the boy did not refuse. "That's a good boy. That's right. Good boy. That makes Grandpa happy."

"He ought to call you Great-Grandpa," the child's father said. "Not Grandpa."

"How am I supposed to remember all that?" the old man said. "Grandpa, Great-Grandpa, it doesn't matter, as long as they call me something. Come here, don't run away."

The older ones continued to evade him.

"Stop running, Jimmy, Helen." The children's mother stopped them by using the English names they'd adopted for their private lessons.

Timothy's mother had used his English name, too, but the three syllables were too hard for the old man to imitate. He did all right with two-syllable names. "Which one is Chimney and which one is Hailing? Come here. Ha-ha." The English names sounded

Taiwanese in his mouth and made everyone laugh, including the old man himself. Then the children laughed when Jimmy and Helen found chicken pieces in their bowls.

"I have no idea how you raised your children. Why don't they like this kind of chicken? I remember how you all looked forward to the New Year's holiday when we offered sacrifices so you could each have a piece of chicken." The old man pointed to his eldest son. "One time we had dinner guests after celebrating a deity's birthday when Ah-shui was about seven. He was standing by the dinner table watching the guests eat, and he began to cry when he saw one of them go back for more chicken. 'He's already had three pieces, but he's taking more. He'll finish it all. What about me?' The guest was so embarrassed."

"What happened after that?" someone asked.

"After that? Well, I took him out back and gave him a beating! What do you think happened?" The old man smiled at Ah-shui, who was now in his fifties and a grandfather himself.

"I don't remember any of that," Ah-shui said with a red face, bringing on another round of laughter. The children, who did not find it funny, thought they must have misunderstood, and they pestered their parents for an explanation. Some of the parents repeated the story patiently, but it still did not seem funny to children for whom the hardships of an earlier time were totally alien.

Kite bells seemed to be getting louder and merrier outside. Rice bowls in hand, the children ran out onto the threshing ground and looked up, yelling with excitement at the sight of one of the kites, though they did not know what it was called. Old Mr. Wu told them it was a centipede and pointed out the rest for them: that one was a double-circle; the one next to it was a hexagon, or eight-corner; and the biggest one was a seventy-two-corner kite. Even with the kites pointed out to them, the children still didn't know what was what, as if the answer from the old man had raised more questions. Convinced that they really needed him, he was overjoyed, even when they pestered him endlessly.

"Ah-pa." Ah-shui came out and called to his father, but the old man seemed deaf. The others inside did not want Ah-shui to get his father, telling him to hang up the phone, which was what he planned to do. But the old man had heard him after all.

Wu Xinyi turned toward the house, perturbed by the absence of cheerfulness in Ah-shui's tone and the way the others were looking at him. "What's wrong?" He sounded tense now as he rushed back inside, under the gaze of the others the whole time.

Ah-que, his oldest son's wife, covered the mouthpiece with one hand. "It's for you." She sounded unhappy with the caller.

"Who is it?" The old man was perplexed.

"Them."

"Who? Them? Who's them?"

"Hua Tianfang's oldest son."

"What does he want to talk to me about?" He walked up.

"I don't know. He just said it was urgent."

"Tell him Papa isn't here. Don't get it." Ah-shui was annoyed. The others agreed.

"We can't say that. They knew we'd all be back today, and that Papa would be home."

"We haven't heard from them in ages. Why are they calling after all this time?" The old man blanched and continued in a panicky voice, "Could something have happened to my mother?" He reached for the phone.

Instead of handing it to him, Ah-que said, "Probably not. Your mother is their mother, too, and he didn't sound like it was about her." She handed him the phone. The children, who had swarmed in to ask the old man to watch the kites with them, were subdued by the tension inside and quickly lost their high spirits. One adult even threatened them, "Don't be pests. Be quiet. If not, Grandpa won't take you out to fly a kite later." That shut them up.

The older children, who were sitting at the two tables in the kitchen, came over to hear what Old Mr. Wu would say to the caller.

"Xinyi here. What's going on?" He saw that everyone was looking at him, so he turned to face the wall. "Did you say you're Kuni? Are you Kuni?" He used his half-brother's Japanese name, like everyone in the other family. The old man turned his face back so his family would know who he was talking to. Of course, they already knew it was someone from Hua Tianfang's family, which was why they did not look too happy. They had not wanted him to take the call; that included the older grandchildren. His children had seen what had happened to him; like their own children, they had heard what had happened in the past, before even they were born, from Old Mr. Wu and his wife, not to mention neighbors and other relatives.

"This can't be good." The grownups were talking among themselves, all trying to keep their voices down so the caller would not hear them.

"Mother wants to see me?" The old man's voice sounded somewhat shrill, with a hint of a quiver. "She wants to come live with me?"

The family members around him raised their voices, no longer worried that the caller would hear them; some even talked louder to make sure they were heard. "Impossible! Hua Tianfang chased Father out." Ah-shui, who had witnessed everything as a youngster, was incensed.

***

"Ah-pa—Ah-pa!" One morning Ah-shui was catching a train to his high school, where he was a first-year student, and spotted Hua Tianfang, who was a head taller than the other passengers from Taipei. He spun around and ran home, shouting as he entered their house. The fright in Ah-shui's voice unnerved Mr. Wu so much that he screamed at his son. "What's gotten into you? Have you been humped by a dog? Why are you shouting like that?"

"Hua Tianfang is here again, Ah-pa. You have to leave." Ah-shui's news sent the family into a panic. The other children, who had been slurping congee at the dining table before heading off to school, were too disconcerted to finish eating. Reminded of the earlier experience, the younger ones even started crying.

"Leave now. Go, go outside. Don't worry about your belt. Just hold up your pants with your hand," Mrs. Wu said.

"I can't. He'll see me. I'll hide behind the kindling upstairs," Mr. Wu said as he picked up the ladder leaning against the wall and turned it around so the top rung met the stairs. After scrambling up, he strained to pull up the ladder and finally managed with his wife's help from down below, shortly before a tall, dark shadow walked in against the light.

"Where's that damn Yi-zai? Get over here, you good-for-nothing," Hua said contemptuously, with no regard for anyone.

Jinyu, Xinyi's wife, blocked his way with her brood of children behind her.

"Yi-zai left early this morning." She pleaded with him softly, "Please don't hit him again. He can't take it."

"You stay out of this, woman," Hua said as he shoved her away and strode in. He went into one of the bedrooms and looked under the bed before searching the kitchen and the toilet. Jinyu took the opportunity to tell Ah-shui to get Mr. Qiu Bao, who had been a district police officer under Japanese rule. "Go find Mr. Qiu, even if it makes you late for school."

After failing to find Xinyi anywhere, Hua sat down in the main room and crossed his legs. "I can't believe I can't find him."

Jinyu made a cup of hot tea and offered it to him solicitously. "Have a cup while you wait. But please don't hit him, I beg you. Don't hit him again. He is, after all, the father of seven now, so don't beat him like before, please." She was on the verge of crying.

"I enjoy it. What are you going to do about it?"

"Please have some tea."

"Please have some tea? Have some tea? Why are you trying to get me to drink? Did you poison the tea?"

"You—" Jinyu forced herself to stop.

"I what?" Tianfang continued to menace her.

"You're terrible," she said, and reached out to take the cup away. He grabbed her hand with lightning speed, spilling the hot liquid on Jinyu, who jerked her hand back and knocked the cup over, drenching his crotch. Like a martial arts master, he leaped into the air and gave her a savage slap across the face when he landed. With a cry, she fell to the floor.

Xinyi, who was hiding out upstairs and even had to fart in increments, called out upon hearing his wife scream when she was slapped. "You can hit me, but leave my wife alone!" He stuck his head out to look over the stairs, anxious to get down to check on her.

"You've got no balls!" Tianfang walked over and shouted up

at him with his hands on his hips. "No one would believe those seven kids came from you. Come down here if you've got the balls."

Jinyu got up and rushed over to the spot below the opening when she heard Xinyi move the ladder to get down. "Don't come down, Xinyi," she sobbed. "Your stepfather is cold-blooded, with no feelings for anyone. Let him say what he wants; it can't hurt you, but he'll beat you to a pulp if you come down."

"Someone like him is better off dead. He's an embarrassment, and there's no point in keeping him around. Come down here, you worthless little shit."

"Listen to me, Yi-zai. Don't come down." The children crowded around their mother and began to cry.

"I haven't beaten him to death yet, so why are you crying? You can wait to mourn him after I kill him. Come on, come down here. Your wife and children have already started the mourning rites, so why not come down and make it real?"

"Are you all right, Jinyu-zai?" Xinyi asked anxiously, eager to get down but afraid of being punched by his stepfather. She said she was fine, though her left cheek burned. "How about the baby?" he added.

"*Your* baby? As if it's yours to worry about!" Tianfang was equally mean with his tongue. "Come down here."

Not wanting her husband to come down for more beatings, she had told him that words from his stepfather couldn't hurt; but after the insult, she would rather suffer more slaps than hear something so scandalous. "I'm all right, Yi-zai. Just don't come down, no matter what."

Even the older children were tearfully telling their father not to come down, a comforting sight to him, for he was reassured that his children did not consider his hiding out to be a cowardly act.

One up and one below. Tianfang could do nothing as long as Xinyi stayed put, so he walked over to the main room to look for a weapon. By this time, more than a dozen grownups from five neighboring families had walked in to corner him in a spot near the door, deflating him somewhat, though he wouldn't relent.

"Family business has to be dealt with by family members. This is between Wu Xinyi and me, and has nothing to do with you. So please leave now."

"Nothing to do with us, you say?" It happened to be a non-slaughtering day, so Yan-zai, the butcher, had been able to come over. The hard-featured man spoke out against the injustice: "Good neighbors are more like blood brothers. Don't you know that? You've gone too far. You're his stepfather, and you beat him because he's not your own. Since Yi-zai moved here over a decade ago, I've seen you beat him often, and today I have to speak up for him or I'm a pig." His comment made everyone laugh, easing the tension in the air while justifying his righteous intervention. "Don't laugh. I'm serious. I have to say something even if you beat me to death," the butcher continued as he turned to glance at his new allies with a pleased look.

The butcher's wife was not in the business of slaughtering pigs, but after nearly three decades of a happy marriage, she looked a lot like her husband, with a similar body shape and hoarse voice. She picked up where her husband had left off: "Mr. Hui." She mispronounced the man's surname, intentionally or not, which added a negative connotation. Everyone laughed again, sharing the impression that the butcher's wife was more aggressive than her husband. Sensing the crowd's sentiment about her, she made good use of the momentum and continued emphatically, "Did you just tell us to leave? Take a look around you. We're in Wu Xinyi's house, and you have no right to tell us to leave. We're all in the same saving club that helped Xinyi buy this house, and it will be a while before the loan is paid off. Put bluntly, this house is ours until that day comes. Are you aware of that?"

At some point, Hua, who had his arms crossed and his head raised in an arrogant, menacing pose, had started inching away, without realizing what he was doing. He was at the doorsill by the time she finished.

Qiu Bao walked in with Ah-shui. Under Japanese rule, Qiu and Hua had gone to the same high school, so Qiu spoke in Japanese the moment he saw Hua. "Are you drunk, Tianfang?"

"No." Tianfang was deflated at the sight of Qiu.

"Then why are you acting like this? Have you no sense of shame?"

Hua uncrossed his arms. The moment Qiu walked in, Hua moved outside, like water overflowing a brimming bowl.

"Come over to my house if you've got a minute. What do you say?" Qiu walked outside after issuing his invitation.

There was no response from Hua, who headed for the train station. People inside came out and pointed at him, speaking loud enough for him to hear them talking about him, but he did not turn his head to look back.

***

While listening to Old Mr. Wu talk on the phone, the others began talking about things they'd witnessed and heard, creating a minor din. Those with loud voices, an elder's status, or a talent for storytelling were able to make themselves heard, and quickly became the centers of small groups of listeners.

"It's only natural and proper for me to bring my mother over if she really wants to live with me. But she's ninety-three, and if you just want to dump her on me because she has serious health problems—" Mr. Wu softened his tone and continued, "No, you listen to me, Kuni. You and your four brothers are her sons, too. She brought you up and then continued to take care of your children. She has cared for two generations of your family. Back then—" He was interrupted again but managed to cut back in. "It's not like that, Kuni. Let me finish. Back then I wanted so much to see her, but you refused no matter how much I begged you. You even said it would be hard because your father was still alive. Let me finish. After your father died, I wanted to go celebrate her eightieth birthday, but none of you would let me. What? A misunderstanding? That can happen only once, but you turned me down every time I asked to see her. And you wouldn't let her come to see me, either. That was inexcusable." The old man's tone changed from protesting to complaining; he was choking up, and his eyes were getting red.

"That's true." The others in the room were getting furious as they talked among themselves and listened to the old man on the phone. The groups were now united in their shared moral outrage. "What a shameless bunch. Once they said they wouldn't come to us even if there was no one left in their family."

***

It was the thirteenth day of the last lunar month, a cold, rainy day. Umbrellas had turned every street in Banqiao into a mushroom garden. Wu Xinyi, followed by his sons who were free that day, along with their wives and children, was on the way to celebrate his mother's eightieth birthday. They had brought for Wu Huang Feng, his mother, a pair of two-ounce gold bracelets, and other symbols of longevity, such as peach-shaped buns, pig's feet in rice noodles, and red-dyed eggs. He thought it was a given that he should want to celebrate her birthday; they had even planned to have a delegation of four generations, but for the fact that the great-grandchildren were away in other cities and overseas. They hadn't expected to be turned down after traveling from Yilan to Banqiao, a journey that had left them drenched below the knees.

"Kuni," the sixty-four-year-old Xinyi knocked on the door and pleaded, "all of us, adults and children, have been waiting here for over an hour. Could you please let us see her and give her our presents? Have Taka or Shige or anyone else come out if you don't want to talk to me."

There was no response from inside. Earlier, through the frosted window, they had been able to see people watching TV inside, but now the lights were off.

"We have to have some backbone, Ah-pa. They don't want us here, so let's go home." Ah-shui held back his anger to talk his father around.

"Yes, let's go back to Yilan," someone echoed.

"What are you saying?" Xinyi was upset. "Today is my mother's eightieth birthday. I can't give up on seeing her because of them. She's my mother, she gave birth to me—" He began to sob. Eyes were reddening and noses aching on his sons and daughters-in-law, and the sadness even had the young grandson wailing in his mother's arms.

"Whoever wants to go home can leave now. That's fine with me, but I have to stay."

None of them dared leave without him, but not because he had been a strict father. Wu and his wife had done a good job raising their children by setting an example themselves. They knew how much their father missed his mother, because they'd heard since childhood how she had raised him; they had also seen with their own eyes how many concessions and sacrifices he had made so she would not be mistreated by the Hua family.

"How can you say that, Ah-pa? You know we won't do that," Ah-shui said. "It's getting late, and there are only two more trains for Luodong today."

Distressed by the information, Xinyi knelt and began to bang on the door. "I don't care what you say. I will kneel here till I die if you won't let me see my mother."

Ah-shui and the others tried to help him up, but he refused. The Hua family was relatively well known in the neighborhood because of their minor wealth in the past. Therefore, the eldest, Guoxiong, or Kuni, opened the door to save face, and explained to the gathering crowd, "Come on, get up. We can't let you do that. We're brothers, after all, even though we have different fathers. Come on, get up."

Xinyi's mood lifted, as he thought the man not only acknowledged him as a half-brother, but had agreed to let him see his mother. He did not know that Guoxiong had more to say. Xinyi reached out to shake hands, but was ignored. "I know what you really want," he said. "You came to celebrate her birthday because you know my mother inherited a large piece of land in Maozailiao, since there is no son in her family."

"What are you talking about?" Xinyi did not know what to say, as he felt the blood rush to his head.

"What am I talking about? I'm saying you're trying to catch a big fish with tiny bait. What else could I be saying?"

"Let's go home, Ah-pa." Ah-shui and Ah-que each put an arm around Xinyi, who lowered his head, with his right hand on his chest. Wordlessly, he let his children take him with them. The downpour continued unabated. They had barely taken a step before the eldest son of the Hua family spat out a warning: "Don't you ever come back to bother us." That was followed by the loud bang of a slammed door. Roused by the noise, Wu Xinyi muttered repeatedly as he crossed the street in the rain, "My heart hurts so badly."

***

The earlier solemn atmosphere in the house could no longer constrain the children listening in on the phone conversation. They began to fidget, despite what their parents said to keep them quiet. Finally, the adults told five of the older kids to take everyone else out into the shade under the eaves to watch the kites. One wanted to watch from the river, but the elders said no.

There were many more kites by then. Through the loudspeakers at the festival ground came descriptions of the kites and the names of their creators, which the children could hear clearly even from inside the fence. "Everyone in the audience, please take note. A rare large kite is about to soar into the sky. Let's cheer it on." Loud applause erupted around the emcee and, magnified by the microphone in her hand and the loudspeakers, came to the children like a string of firecrackers tossed into the sky. They clapped happily to echo the festivities beyond the fence.

"Wow!" the emcee shouted in surprise. "It's flying. It's in the air. It's huge. What an incredible, marvelous kite." She did not ask the audience to clap, but the applause this time was even more exuberant, sounding like a fish being lowered into a hot, smoky wok. Having only heard but not seen the splendid kite taking flight, the Wu children could not bring themselves to applaud; instead they craned their necks and waited. Following the applause outside, the head of a kite bobbed above the tips of the bamboo fence, but the children still could not tell what they were looking at. A gust of wind sent the kite up over the green waves of bamboo leaves and into the sky. Now applause erupted inside the fence as the audience outside stopped clapping.

"A big bird." "A peacock." The children rattled off their guesses.

"What you're seeing now, everyone, is a rarity called a phoenix. An average kite will take flight as long as the two sides are symmetrical. But symmetry won't work for a phoenix, because it needs to leap, spread its wings, bring in its feet, and display its tail. It's hard to create a kite that will do all of that and still fly steadily."

As the kite was lifted by the wind, the kite flyer began letting out the line; if the kite dipped to the point of falling, he halted the reel and tugged the line to send it up again.

"Attention, everyone. The phoenix was saved for last because it can soar higher than any of the others. Now I'm going to tell you about the kite master, a national treasure, who made this one. His name is You Xiangrui, from Tamsui, and he's seventy-four years old." It was clear that the emcee was reading a script. "The phoenix took him a month to finish, and we hear that he fell ill from the exhausting work. He was not able to fly the kite himself today." Her voice became emotional: "Oh, it's so touching. I sincerely hope that old Mr. You will recover soon."

The kite flyer must have let out more line, for the bird was rising higher and looking smaller, drawing an excited shout from the emcee. "Mr. You's phoenix is rising into the sky again. A round of applause, everyone. Old Mr. You is flying into the sky." With her free hand she was tapping the hand holding the microphone, mingling applause with a thumping sound like someone beating a blanket. In a peevish but somewhat amused voice, a man shouted, "Please turn off the mike, Miss Chen."

"Why?"

"Turn it off." The sound was now right beside her. Convinced that the microphone was off, the man said, "Earlier you said old Mr. You, the kite master, had fallen ill from the effort of creating the phoenix. And just now you said he was rising into the sky. That's an awful thing to say."

"Oh!" The emcee emitted a muffled cry, likely with her hand over her mouth, which was broadcast by the loudspeakers.

The older children in the Wu family burst out laughing, but the younger ones were mystified. One of the older kids laughed his way into the main room, where, ignoring the tension inside, he continued laughing and said, "That's so funny."

"Stop that. Grandpa is on the phone." The boy's father glared at him.

"But I want to tell you something really funny—"

"Not now." His father pointed outside. The boy left without another word.

Old Mr. Wu's tone was starting to soften. His remaining resistance reflected the fact that members of his family were silently or vocally expressing their opposition to continuing the phone conversation and the relationship with the other family.

"It's not just me. My children and grandchildren are grown now, and they must not be laughed at because of my actions. No. You listen to me. Do you understand what I'm saying? You do? All right."

"Kuni?" Ah-shui asked. Mr. Wu nodded.

"Tell him to have some backbone and act like a man. He has to think about what you did for them when they were young and how they treated you after they grew up." Ah-shui's complaint was loud enough for the caller to hear.

"Yes, that was Ah-shui," Mr. Wu continued. "You can't blame them. They've seen how your family treated me. Not just me—them too. What's in the past? I'm not a great man like Jesus or as compassionate as Mazu. I'm human. What? Right, you're a man, a despicable man."

"Why say so much to him?" People in the room thought that Old Mr. Wu had already fallen into a trap, while at the other end they were afraid he would stop talking to them; as long as they could keep him talking, they had a chance of getting what they wanted.

"None of the five sons in that family is any good, especially the oldest one, Kuni. He said he was studying in Japan, attending Waseda University, but instead he was whoring and drinking his days away. He even managed to deceive their father, Hua Tianfang." Ah-shui's temper was rising.

"Their last name is Hua, as in 'huahua gonzi,' a playboy, so what else would he do but go whoring?" Ah-wen, the third son, added jocularly.

***

Three years after Hua Guoxiong had lied to his father about studying in Japan, a quarrel broke out between Xinyi and his wife one night, the first for the couple. She cried all night, and he could not sleep. "No matter how bad he is, he's my brother, from the same mother." Hua Guoxiong had sent another telegram from Tokyo asking for help, with a request that Xinyi keep it from his father, Hua Tianfang. Unable to come up with the requested amount quickly, Xinyi had pleaded with Jinyu to sell her dowry and her annual presents from him, including gold rings, necklaces, bracelets, and earrings. He would then go to Japan to help Guoxiong, though he had no idea what sort of jam his half-brother might be in.

"Let's consider it a loan. How's that? I'll pay you back a little at a time, with interest."

"What are you saying? You make it sound like I'm fussing over money. I'm just worried. We don't know about the two younger ones yet, but the older three, especially Guoxiong, are like a bottomless pit. You can never fill it up no matter how much money you dump in. Is it worth it, what you're doing?"

"I don't think about whether it's worth it or not. He's in trouble, and I have to do my best. That's all I think about."

"You've done your best every time. And that's precisely why it's getting out of hand. You said the same thing about Hua Tianfang, calling him your father because of your mother. He took what you made as a broker and notary; he got the titles to the land and house you bought and sold it piece by piece." A rooster crowed outside. Jinyu stopped crying when it touched upon the land and the house; her tone of voice made it sound to him as if she were choking. That hurt.

"Would you stop it?" He sounded upset.

Without a word, she got out of bed, opened a drawer, and came back with a small wooden chest, which she laid down next to him. "It's all in here. But you have to let me finish before you take it."

"What do you mean, Jinyu?" He took her hands as he drew close so he could see her face in the dim light.

"Don't overthink it." She laughed softly. "I'm not going to kill myself. I won't do that. I'm not irresponsible, and I want to see our children grow up."

That brought tears to Xinyi's eyes. His head drooped, like a little boy facing his mother. She freed her hands and then held his, gently touching her forehead against the top of his head.

"I accumulated enough good karma in my previous life to marry someone like you. I'm not sure there's another one like you in the world, but there's a limit to being a good person. I'm sure you're aware that your stepfather has another family of seven or eight in Shulin. Everyone, including our family, is dependent on you for survival. You could have three heads and six arms, but it's getting to the point that you can't take it much longer. When a silkworm is young, it can live on a few mulberry leaves, but you can't give it enough leaves once it's ready to make a cocoon. It's the same with people. If you keep helping them out like this, they will chew your bones up and spit them out. You give him money, while his father beats you—"

Xinyi was getting sadder and sadder, shedding tears and sniffling. "I was just hoping he'd spare Mother if I gave him money."

"I know that. I also know he'd vent his anger on your mother because of you."

"Our poor mother." Xinyi was sobbing.

"Don't cry. Don't let the children hear you cry. It's almost light out and you haven't slept a wink, so lie back down and sleep for a couple hours. I'm getting up to make breakfast for the children before they go to school."

He lay down, pulled the blanket over his head, and wept. She patted the blanket and let out a long sigh, so long that she was nearly out of breath.

***

The children watching the kites were laughing and clapping spiritedly, creating a racket that surged into the main room like a tidal wave.

"Papa—Mama, come look at the Mazinger!"

"Come see Mazinger."

One of the mothers missed what her son was saying. Afraid that they were making too much noise for the adults inside, she went out to quiet them down. Following the children's gaze, she looked up and saw the kite, a replica of the anime Mazinger, swaying from side to side as it struggled to take flight.

"Needless to say, the children all know what this kite is," the emcee was saying. "Yes, that's Mazinger." Through the loudspeakers they could hear the excited shouts from the adults and children standing near the microphone.

Unlike its anime original, this Mazinger not only looked clumsy, but seemed to have trouble flying. The Wu family children watched it rocking above the bamboo fence leaves, where it waited for a gust of wind. Up it went, but it continued to sway from side to side. The phoenix, in contrast, was poised high above the other kites, like a mighty sovereign towering over its subjects, as if it were the center of the universe.

"Everyone, this Mazinger kite is having trouble flying, despite the shouts of the children cheering it on. It is very heavy. Its maker, Mr. Fang Jie, says he won't let the children down and will make adjustments to send it high into the sky." She had barely finished when the audience saw the line being pulled in and the kite beginning to fall.

One of the children thought about his mother after the kite's failed attempt to take flight and ran back inside, followed by others about the same age. The main room felt even grimmer than before. Why was their grandpa or great-grandpa looking so sad on the phone, they asked their parents, who gestured for them to keep quiet.

"It's been twenty, thirty years, and she's never said she wanted to see me. Why now?" Old Mr. Wu needed to be convinced. "All right, I won't hang up. You go get her to talk to me." Still with the handset against his ear, he said to his children with an anxious and agitated look, "My mother is going to talk to me. It's been more than thirty years since they chased me out, and Hua Tianfang wouldn't let us see each other. We never even had a chance to talk on the phone. She might have agreed not to get in touch with me. Once, before they moved to Banqiao, she asked a vegetable vendor to pass along a secret message, telling me she'd been forced to stop contacting me for my sake. Otherwise—" Thinking that someone was on the phone, he called out excitedly, "Hello! It's me, Yi-zai. Hello? Hello!" He was too tense; no one was on the phone yet.

"Take it easy. Don't get so worked up," one of his children said.

"We, we haven't spoken in more than thirty years." A smile creased his tear-streaked face. "Why is it taking them so long?"

"Don't be too anxious. She's in her nineties. It will take her a while to walk from her room to the living room."

"Ninety-three. I heard she's still in good health, just hard of hearing. You have to shout for her to hear you. But she can't recall anything that's happened over the past forty or fifty years; that's her only problem. I'm the only one she can remember. She still uses my childhood name, Foolish Yi-zai. She told them she wanted to see Foolish Yi-zai."* Someone appeared to have come to the phone, so he gripped the handset and shouted, "Hello! Auntie—this is Foolish Yi-zai." His face fell. "Didn't you say you'd have Mother come to the phone?"

---

*It would not have been uncommon for a son to call his mother "Auntie" in an earlier, traditional family in Taiwan. Old Mr. Wu might have been forced to give up calling her "Mother" when she remarried.

The others laughed when they realized it wasn't his mother.

"Kuni! Don't lie to me. Do you remember what you said to me that time in Japan?"

***

Jinyu had given Xinyi all her jewelry to help Guoxiong out in Japan. When he got there, the situation was worse than he'd imagined. His half-brother not only wasn't attending college, but he had been supporting a girl who worked in a small tavern. The bar girl, Chiko, was pregnant with his baby.

"Guoxiong, your family has sent you money for tuition and living expenses over the past three years, and I've secretly sent you money whenever you needed more. But *this* is how you spent your money!"

"Elder Brother, please don't tell Father. I can get a diploma with a little more money, and I'll be able to earn a living when I return to Taiwan."

"What are you going to do about Chiko?"

"There are two possibilities. One, I'll need to get money for an abortion and accept a settlement. Her family lives in the poor Aomori Prefecture. It'll be easy to deal with country folks like them, so we won't have to spend too much. Two, I'll marry her and take her back to Taiwan. Marrying a Japanese, like having a diploma, will earn us respect." Guoxiong smiled smugly.

"You're shameless."

"I know I screwed up, Older Brother. Please help me out this time, just this once. I'll be eternally grateful. You know what? You'll always feel more like a father to me."

"Don't talk like that."

Xinyi did a quick calculation after he came home; it would take all of Jinyu's jewelry, plus a house, to pay off Guoxiong's debt and settlement with the girl's family. With Hua Tianfang owning the deed to all the properties, Xinyi decided to sell a house by Yilan's North Gate without telling Hua. Guoxiong was able to spend another year in Japan to maintain the appearance of finishing four years of college. He then married Chiko and brought her back after the abortion. Xinyi made up a story about a failed investment when Hua found out about the sale of the house. And because of that, he seized everything Xinyi owned. Worse yet, he demanded the money from the house sale and beat Xinyi whenever he felt like it. He even took the train back to Yilan to do that after moving to Banqiao. The money Xinyi had given him over the years ended up being more than the house was worth, but Hua kept coming back for more, and the abuse never let up.

***

"Come on, Ah-pa, you've talked to him enough," Ah-shui said, but the old man ignored him.

"That's what people mean by blindly loyal and foolishly filial," Mingde, the oldest of the grandsons and a teacher, commented.

"That's so true. He'd give up his life for her if he had to."

"We'll never understand his feelings for his mother. There was a time when they nearly starved to death." Ah-shui knew his father best.

"Mazinger!" The children watching the kite outside shouted. "Mazinger!"

The kite managed to take off this time, but it looked different; it was now buoyed by a large balloon on its head and one on each of its shoulders.

"Mazinger is flying again, everyone," the emcee started up again. "It's based on Mr. Fang's original design, but the three added balloons are a violation of the rules of the competition, so he is disqualified. He can still participate because the organizers don't want to disappoint all the children who are eager to see Mazinger. An exception has been made, so we must thank the organizers and Mr. Fang."

Amid the lackluster applause, the kite went up, still swaying violently from side to side; at some point one of the balloons popped, sending the kite listing to the right and heading toward the phoenix.

"Please move the Mazinger kite away," the emcee said.

Then the balloon on its head popped. With only one balloon left, the kite lost its balance completely and entangled the line of the phoenix. The kites around it could not escape, either, and fell in an intertwined mess along with the Mazinger.

"Oh, no!" the emcee shouted. "Ai! They've all fallen into the river."

One child took it so hard he ran in and shouted, "The Mazinger and the phoenix fell into the water with some other kites."

"Shush." A grownup sitting by the door put his arm around the child.

"I want Mama." The child tried to push the arm away, straining to escape. But everyone in the main room heard him and turned to give him an ugly look, so frightening him that he tried even harder to find his mother.

"Jimmy!" his mother warned in a low voice. She did not look happy.

"Mama." The child finally made it to his mother, after passing several grownups sitting in chairs and then crawling under the table. She told him to keep quiet, so he pulled her head down and put his hand on her neck to whisper into her ear. That calmed him down.

Old Mr. Wu's hands were shaking. Someone brought him a chair and said, "Take it easy."

"I think they mean it this time." He sat down. "We haven't spoken in more than thirty years."

His children tried not to laugh at hearing this again, but some could not quite manage it.

"It's true. We, we haven't spoken in more than thirty years."

They all laughed emotionally this time.

"Be quiet." Old Mr. Wu could hear Kuni and some other people over the phone. They were telling the old lady to take it slow. They sounded so close, he could not sit still. "Here she comes. They're bringing her over and telling her not to hurry," he said, like giving a live broadcast. "Oh. Not a word from you. Hello? Hello? This is Foolish Yi-zai." He quickly recovered from the excitement. "Kuni, did you bring her over? I heard it. Good, very good. That's good. Give it to her." He was getting nervous again.

"Sit down, take your time."

Wu had barely sat down before he stood back up, nudging the stool backward with his thighs and overturning it. "Hello! Auntie? Are you Auntie? Hello? Hello? Are you Auntie? I'm Foolish Yi-zai." Tears welled up in his eyes again as he turned to say, "I can hear her, why can't she hear me?"

"Don't worry and take it slow. Call her Auntie and tell her who you are. Don't *ask* her if she's Auntie."

"Hello! Kuni. What's going on? I was talking to her, but then nothing. How come? Yes, I heard her voice. Oh, all right. All right." The old man turned to explain: "She doesn't remember anything and doesn't know we can talk over the phone. Kuni is going to hold the handset for her. Good, she's here. We haven't spoken in more than thirty years."

"Why don't you sit down to talk to her?"

He couldn't.

"Hello! All right." He responded to Kuni before saying to his mother, "Auntie, this is Foolish Yi-zai. Do you remember me? Yes, Foolish Yi-zai. I was born in Maozailiao. Do you remember the place? Yes, right, Maozailiao. Right. Oh, you recall the flood? Yes, the house was washed away. Yes, we ate sweet potatoes and vines that were meant for the pigs. Oh, you remember so much."

Mr. Wu was laughing and crying at the same time. "You don't know where you are? You're living in Banqiao with Kuni. You don't know them? Where am I? I live in Dongguashan. Who am I? I'm your oldest son, Foolish Yi-zai. Don't you remember me? Yes, I'm Foolish Yi-zai. Once I cried and refused to eat a sweet potato. I threw it to the floor and you hit me. I cried and so did you. I do remember that. How could I forget?

"You don't know where you are? Sure, sure, I'll come bring you home. When? I'll be there tonight. I will. I know how to get there. I'll be there.

"No, no need to take the ferry anymore. Everything is different now. Su Gongchui, the ferryman, died.

"I've told you already. I'm your oldest son, Foolish Yi-zai. I'm listening. Go ahead. No, I won't tell anyone.

"Of course I know my birth father. His name was Wu Quan. I know. He died of dysentery.

"Poisoned? Hua Tianfang? …"

"Hello? Hello?" His mother's voice disappeared, so he kept shouting into the phone until someone came back on the line. "Hello? Is that you, Kuni? Where's my mother? A problem with her head? Talking nonsense? But she remembered everything from the past clearly. Well, don't you want me to bring her here to live with me? I'll come to Banqiao a little later. Someone will take me. We'll be there before nightfall. You'll wait for me at home? Good. Good. Give me a call if anything comes up. Sure, sure. I know." He put down the phone and said emotionally, "I didn't expect to have a chance to see my mother again. We haven't seen each other in more than thirty years. Almost forty years. Such a long time, don't you think?"

"Ah-pa, do you really want to bring Grandma back to live with you?" Ah-shui was apprehensive.

"What do you think?" When no one answered, he said, "I know this is a tough decision for you, but for me it's very simple. I'm her son, and I can only say yes if she wants to come live with me. Besides, think about it. She doesn't know whose house it is and where she is, so she wants to see me and move back here. I'm sure it won't be easy, but I'm her son."

"We're not really against it, but the Hua family shouldn't have picked this moment to send her back, since it's the children's responsibility to take care of the mother. If I may be so blunt, you need someone to care for you, too," Mingde said.

"That's not a problem. Think positively; this is a family reunion. We offer up our respects to the ancestors on the Double-Ninth holiday. The ancestors returned, and nearly every member of the younger generations is back. And now we're in touch with my mother, your grandma or great-grandma, for some of you your great-great-grandma. Isn't this a wonderful family reunion?" Old Mr. Wu looked delighted. "We owe that to our ancestors and to my wife, your grandma."

His children and grandchildren did not share his view, but they decided not to bring up all the potential problems now that his wish had finally been granted.

Mingde offered to drive his grandpa to Banqiao to meet Great-Grandma, describing her amnesia in later life as a self-imposed escapist forgetfulness. In his view, Great-Grandma had married Hua Tianfang so that her son would not have to eat sweet potatoes every day, never expecting that he would be worked like a beast of burden and abused by the Hua family even though he was no longer hungry. She could do nothing to improve his life because she herself was in a precarious situation. Hua Tianfang had married her simply for her looks.

"That's true. She was like a fairy in rags when she was young, and she looked like a fairy godmother as she got older," the old man said with pride when he recalled his mother's appearance.

"A fairy is pretty, but a fairy godmother?" someone said in jest, making everyone laugh.

"It's an analogy. She's ninety-three, but I believe she still has her looks, just as before," Mr. Wu said as something from the past flashed through his mind. It was the spring before Hua had run him out of the house. Hua had installed a woman called Wurou in Shulin. When Xinyi's mother heard about it, she asked Hua if it was true, and he hit and kicked her. Xinyi went up to protect his mother, so Hua beat him, too. But he was emboldened by the need to keep his mother safe.

"You should have no complaints about my mother. She does everything in this house, and she's prettier than other women."

Tianfang's rage turned to amusement. "What's good is being pretty?" he said with a laugh. "She's like a coffin board in bed. I'm not a pig that wants to mount a bench."

Huang Feng jumped to her feet and ran to the back of the house.

"What's wrong? You don't like the sound of that? Well, Wurou moans and groans in bed, with lots of trashy talk. Heh-heh-heh." Hua turned to a dazed Xinyi and said, "You're too young to understand. A woman like your mother should be a nun."

***

The elation on Mr. Wu's face had vanished.

"Ah-pa, from your conversation with your mother, it seems that Hua Tianfang may have poisoned your father. Can that be true?" Ah-shui asked. "That's a serious accusation. Your grandma's losing her mind, so it can't be true, can it?"

Mr. Wu went quiet before adding, "I think she's losing her mind."

"But I thought she only forgot her later life. She remembers earlier days clearly, doesn't she?" Ah-que asked.

"That's true. So what do you think I should do?" No one answered him, so he continued. "What do I do? Hua Tianfang is long dead, and his bones are dry enough to beat a drum. What can we do?"

"We're not talking about doing anything. It was mentioned over the phone, so I was just curious," Ah-que explained.

Mr. Wu knew that his children did not mean for him to pursue criminal responsibility for his own father's death.

The telephone rang again. Being closest to the phone, the old man picked it up after the first ring. "Hello. This is—"

He listened to the caller, nodding and saying "yes" and "sure" the whole time. It was a couple of minutes before he had a chance to cut in. "Tomorrow, the morning is better. All right, then. Sure, sure." He hung up and said, "Kuni said Mother cried after talking to me on the phone. He said she hasn't cried like that in a long time. She's sleeping now, so he wants us not to go over today. It's too late and she's in bed, so it will be too much trouble. He told us to go tomorrow morning, which will give them time to get everything ready for her. Can you still drive me over there, Mingde?"

"Sure. It's a two-day weekend."

The weather was nice the next day, with refreshing autumn air and a clear blue sky. It was only nine o'clock, and no one working for the kite-flying contest had arrived, but the kites were up, their bells ringing. The Mazinger that had fallen into the river was up again, looking lighter and less unwieldy. It soared steadily upward, catching everyone's attention. Mingde's boy asked his father to roll down the car window so he could stick his head out for a better look.

"Ah, the Mazinger has been changed, and now it doesn't have its sword." The boy searched the sky. "Oh, the pretty phoenix isn't here today."

"That's enough. Keep your head in. We're getting on the highway now."

"When will we get there, Mingde?" the old man asked as he busily stuffed money into red envelopes.

"Around noon."

"That's no good. They'll be having lunch."

"It's all right. They know we're coming, and they'll be ready for us."

They arrived shortly after noon, just as Mingde had said. Unlike his usual self, Kuni was courteous. Xinyi wanted to see his mother right away. "Have a cup of tea and rest up. Then we'll have lunch." Seeing that Xinyi would not sit down, Guoxiong said, "She's in the back room. She just went in to rest. Come, I'll show you."

Leaving Mingde and the boy in the living room, Mr. Wu followed his half-brother to the back room. The door was open, with an old curtain as a screen.

"Do you remember this curtain?" Guoxiong whispered.

"Of course, there's a pair of Mandarin ducks embroidered on it, and the inscription 'A Couple Lives in Harmony.'"

"The curtain and a used chamber pot are the only things that can convince her this is her home. We point at them whenever she wants to go home. But the trick doesn't work anymore, because now she wants to go back to Maozailiao, where she says there's a loofa gourd trellis. She doesn't recall anything else." Guoxiong quietly parted the curtain for Xinyi to peer inside. Mr. Wu saw his mother brushing her hair by a dressing table. A few loose strands were sparklingly white, like silvery light. He pulled the curtain apart to call out softly "Auntie" three times but got no response.

"She's hard of hearing."

Wu walked in and stood behind her, looking at her back and at her face in the mirror. She was still a pretty woman, just as he had said to his family the day before.

"Auntie."

She still didn't hear him, but she saw his face in the mirror and smiled. She turned around and said, "This hotel keeps their windows open all the time. Look, there's often a pretty girl smiling at me."

Mr. Wu got down on his knees, and when she turned around to face him, he shouted, "Auntie, it's me, Foolish Yi-zai." Overcome with emotion, he began to cry, but she pushed his hands off her knees and chided him, "A man must have backbone. And don't go around calling a stranger your mother."

"I'm Foolish Yi-zai."

"What?" she asked. "Louder."

"Ka-san," Guoxiong cut in, "he's Elder Brother, Xinyi-zai. You remember him, don't you?"

"I'm Foolish Yi-zai, your son." Wu got up to speak into her ear.

"You think I don't know what my son looks like? My Foolish Yi-zai is much younger than you."

"I talked to you on the phone yesterday. You said you wanted to go home, and I'm here to take you there. I'm Foolish Yi-zai."

"I know Yi-zai is coming to take me home. Did he send you?"

"I'm Yi-zai, and I'm here to take you home."

"No, no. I can't leave with just anyone. I left with a man called Hua Tianfang years ago, and I suffered for the rest of my life. I won't be foolish like that again. Hee-hee," she laughed.

"Let's have some lunch, Ka-san," Guoxiong said.

Wu was able to hold his emotions in check, but not his tears.

"People are so nice these days. I don't know them, and yet they feed me and don't charge me anything for living here. They also treat me well. People are so much nicer than before." The old lady turned to glance at her dressing table. "See that? The girl outside is looking at me again." She picked up two strings of plastic beads that the Hua children had been playing with. "The guests at this hotel are so careless. Look, they leave valuable pearl and agate necklaces lying around like this. I wonder why they don't come back for them."

Mr. Wu racked his brain to test his mother's memory. "Foolish Yi-zai said he ate so many sweet potatoes as a child that he couldn't stand them any longer. He cried every time he saw potatoes on the table."

"That's true, but there was nothing we could do. I went to borrow money from his uncle. Back then, everyone in Maozailiao ate sweet potatoes. He and I were born with terrible luck, so we had to eat sweet potatoes at every meal for years. But fortunately there's a drop of dew on every blade of grass, and there's always hope. We survived."

"Come, let's go have lunch." Guoxiong reached for her hand, but she refused to move.

"You go eat now. I'm not hungry yet. Go, go on now. This is a woman's room, and men should not stay too long. Go out now so no one will gossip."

Mr. Wu had to laugh despite his grief.

"You can't get her to do anything unless she wants to. Let's go eat. We'll talk about this later."

"Auntie, we'll go eat now."

"Go, go on out."

On their way out, Xinyi said to his half-brother in the hallway, "You've taken good care of Mother, Kuni, and it's been hard. Thank you."

"It's nothing. That's what I should do."

"You ran a tavern when you first came back with Chiko. I heard you later shut it down and opened a pool parlor."

"To be frank with you, the pool parlor lost money, too, so I turned it into a Ping-Pong parlor." They stood by the dining table, and he continued, "Lucky for me, my second daughter married an overseas Chinese from Malaysia. They have a huge lumber business, and she's my source of livelihood. Come have a seat. I'll go get the others over for lunch."

"Mingde is my oldest grandson, Ah-shu's son. He's a teacher," Mr. Wu said as he sat down. "The boy is one of my great-grandsons. I brought them with me to meet Mother."

"Good. I'll go get them now."

Chiko brought out a bowl of soup from the kitchen. Mr. Wu greeted her in polite Japanese, unaware that she was now fluent in Taiwanese. "We haven't seen each other for a long time, and I've changed a lot," she responded in Taiwanese, and they both laughed.

"It's been tough on you caring for Mother. You're doing a great job; it must be hard."

"It's nothing. The old lady has always been neat and takes good care of herself, and she helps out whenever she can. But she's been very forgetful lately and doesn't know who we are anymore."

Mingde and the boy came in, followed by the old lady, who wanted to watch TV in the living room.

"Come have lunch, Auntie."

"I want to watch a movie. You go ahead; don't wait for me." As she walked, she supported herself with one hand on the wall. Mr. Wu had thought she'd be happy to meet her grandson and great-grandson, but he decided not to introduce them when he realized that she didn't even recognize her own son.

"Come, sit down and eat. I'll go turn on the TV for her. Go ahead; I'll be right back." Guoxiong followed his mother out.

"We told her that's TV, but she keeps calling it movies. I sincerely hope I won't be like that when I'm old," Chiko said.

"What does she watch?"

"News!"

"News?"

"Yes. She doesn't watch anything else, not even Taiwanese operas. She just loves watching TV news. Sometimes I try to change the channel when she isn't watching, but she won't let me. It doesn't matter if it's in Mandarin or Taiwanese; she'll watch as long as it's a news program."

"Mother loves watching news programs," Guoxiong walked in and said with a smile. "I turn on an hourly cable news program for her so she can watch as much as she wants."

It was one in the afternoon. The first story on the hourly news program was an exclusive. The old lady focused her attention on the newscaster's face and clothes. The female newscaster said in an excited voice, "Times have truly changed, everyone. A 7-Eleven in Zhonghe was robbed by a woman at two o'clock this morning. The clerk wasn't too concerned about the robber because she was a woman and he was so much bigger and taller, but he was quickly thrown to the floor by the skilled robber. Luckily she fled without taking any money. It was caught on tape, and the police say she won't be hard to find."

Women didn't normally know hand-to-hand combat, which was probably why the news program showed the footage of the women's clean, quick movements three times. The old lady didn't seem to see it, however, as she got to her feet and, facing inside, mumbled to herself, "Well. You told me you'd get my Foolish Yi-zai to come take me home, but you lied to me and got someone else. I'm not stupid. I learned my lesson after Hua Tianfang deceived me. I can go back myself if no one will take me there. I'll go out and get a three wheeler to take me to the ferry landing. And when I get to the landing, the ferryman, Su Gongchui, will ferry me to the loofa gourd trellis. My house is inside the bamboo fence by the trellis." No one paid her any attention since they couldn't hear her over the television volume. She called out anyway, "Thank you very much, proprietor. Thanks for everything. I'm going home now." And with that, she opened the door and walked out onto the busy street.

1999

A Platform With No Timetable

In November 1995, I spent a few days in the Otsuka area in Tokyo to make a protest documentary about six thousand Japanese hemophiliacs who had been infected with the HIV virus through blood products.

The stores on the streets of Otsuka, a residential district in a metropolitan area, carried mostly practical items for daily use, and the coffee shops looked well worn, unlike those in business districts with their fancy décor and ambient lighting. The coffee shops in Otsuka opened early, offering breakfast sandwiches. In terms of price and service, they were a bit like Taiwan's breakfast eateries, but not as busy.

A frosty wind blew outside that morning; with the chilly air, people on the street wore scarves around their necks or turned up the collars of their overcoats and scrunched their necks down. I found a coffee shop near the inn where I was staying. I thought I had walked into the wrong sort of place when I opened the door, but as I was about to turn and leave, the owner invited me to take a seat. For a moment, the sight before me jarred with my experience with coffee shops, since the customers there were gray-haired old folks. Granted, I wasn't all that young myself, but it was impossible not to notice their age. This was more like a private club for senior citizens.

I sat down at a table for two by the door, feeling unnecessarily intrusive. The owner, who looked to be about my age, came over with a menu and a rag to take my order while clearing away the cups and plates from previous customers. I asked for a tuna sandwich combo. Before walking off, he told me that smoking was allowed and brought me an ashtray from the next table. I wondered why he did that. Did he know I was a smoker? Or was he trying to show me that his shop was different from the others? Or did he think I minded because I had looked at the customers who were smoking? He was already back behind the counter opening a can of tuna when I turned to look at him.

The dozen or so customers were bundled up, and in that dimly lit, smoky space it would have been hard to see their faces if it hadn't been for the flickering light of a 29-inch TV set to the left of the counter, on which the NHK morning news was showing. I could only see the outlines of the faces in the corners, while the eyes and their buttons were visible on people facing the TV; their hair was lit up like the flowers on silver grass under a late autumn starry sky.

At first I thought they must have gathered in the shop for companionship, but they didn't seem all that close to one another. They sat in groups of two or three based simply on the way the tables and chairs were laid out, and there were only occasional conversations. Some looked like photosensitive plants, blankly facing the fluorescent light from the TV, oblivious to what was on the screen. The only lively customer was an old woman who, with her face to the wall, was muttering to herself, laughing, sometimes gesturing, as if engaged in an argument. With these groups gathered in but not sharing the small space, it felt colder than outside, almost bone-chilling.

My sandwich came, brought by the obese owner, who walked around the TV to reach my table. In the screen's flickering light, the outlines of the other diners, especially those who got up to move around, appeared flimsy and faint, like lonely souls traveling between the past and the present. As the owner stood in front of me, I saw a pair of sallow, dry, wrinkled hands tucked into the sleeves of his cable-knit sweater. I hadn't noticed them before. I would have found it hard to talk to him if he hadn't worn a smile and had a soft, pleasant voice.

"I'm sorry to have made you wait so long."

"Not a problem. Business is good here."

"It's all because of customers like yourself. They're the usual ones around this time of the day." He glanced at the diners. "A few have yet to show up." He paused and continued with a faint smile. "I'm not sure. Maybe they'll be here."

"You're here alone?"

"Yes. It's too much for one person. Please don't be upset if you find anything lacking. Well, I'll leave you to enjoy your breakfast."

"Today isn't a work day, is it?" I asked, but too late, because he had started to walk away. He turned and came back to my table. "You're right, it's Sunday, and I'd like to take a break, but they'd have no place for breakfast if I closed on Sundays." He walked off with a smile, and soon his shadow passed by the TV to reach the counter.

My eyes had finally adjusted to the dim light, enabling me to see the wrinkles on the faces of those nearest to me, and to hear a few exchanges from the two men at the next table.

"Japan is losing its prowess. These days Japan can't make an atomic bomb to drop on Washington, D.C. We should bomb D.C." He strained to put some force into his outburst.

His tablemate said nothing in response. The speaker turned and our eyes met, and he said to me instead, "I'm right, don't you think? Bomb Washington, D.C."

I responded with a wordless smile, probably making him think that I agreed with him, as he turned to face me. The old man sitting across from him got up, walked past me, opened the door, and left. I was troubled by what I'd seen: not only had he forgotten to zip his fly, but his old pecker was peeking out. Trying not to alert the others, I walked up to the counter and told the owner in a whisper.

"Not again!" he laughed. He put aside what he was doing and ran after the old man. Curious, I followed him out to watch them by the door. The owner called out repeatedly to the old man, though I couldn't tell what he was saying, and the old man finally stopped. I watched the owner walk up, squat down, and zip his fly for him. But instead of getting up right away, he seemed to be struggling, with one hand on the ground to support his tilting body. Then he put both hands on the ground while the old man backed off and reached out to help him to his feet. The owner was already standing with his hands in the old man's by the time I ran past several stores to reach them.

"You're too fat," the old man said.

"Yes, I am." The owner smiled. "Be careful."

"I know."

I was as far as two stores away from them. They bowed repeatedly; it took more than five bows before they finally parted ways. The owner walked back and nodded his apology when he saw me. "He was my primary school principal." He was still panting hard. "I wouldn't have been able to get up without his help."

I went back to my untouched breakfast. When I picked up the tuna sandwich, I saw that the bread wasn't trimmed and that the two pieces weren't even, with the tuna and a slice of tomato peeking out. Without thinking, I looked up at the owner, who seemed to have been watching me. He smiled and nodded. With so much advance apology and overflowing politeness, even the pickiest customer would have forgiven him. Of course, I wasn't bothered by the quality of the service, as my thoughts wandered into this symbiotic corner of Japanese society, where the owner and the old folks depended on each other for their livelihood.

I ate breakfast at the coffee shop four mornings in a row. I picked a table closer to the counter on the last day, when I had more time after finishing my work. The owner chatted with me when he wasn't busy. He told me he had no one else, and that he had serious health issues, just like his aging customers. Like them, he lived one day at a time; they were all waiting.

"I open up to wait for them." His eyes swept past the customers. "They're here hoping for news from their children, waiting on their pensions and the occasional visit from a charitable organization. They come for breakfast and to see each other." He shook his head and continued, "In fact, all they're doing is filling time with pipe dreams, which they shouldn't be doing, since they rely on others for their happiness."

I didn't know how to respond, except to give him a gentle, sad nod, but that didn't seem appropriate. It looked to me as though everyone there was ready for something; they were waiting, with nothing else to do. I looked at my watch, and it was time for my next appointment, so I said to him, "Come visit Taiwan."

To my surprise, the old man sitting at the next table said with a smile, "I will, in my next life."

2000

Listen to Me, All You Deities

Chunmu went to his old friend's funeral one morning and nearly died of envy when he saw Tianfu's six daughters crying their hearts out. He went home right after he'd offered his respects with sticks of incense. The friendship between the two men would normally have required Chunmu to stay until the funeral procession left the house and then walk alongside the coffin for a while. He should have waited to leave until Tianfu's family had thanked all those who came, which was what he had planned to do.

On his way home, he reproached himself for leaving early and thought about Tianfu's daughters, who had sobbed over the loss of their father. He recalled the self-satisfied look on his friend's face in the photo of the deceased. He was reminded of the time a while ago when Tianfu had offered him some betel nuts on the bridge over the irrigation ditch in front of the temple: "Those six girls of mine are terrible. They won't let me drink, smoke, or chew betel nuts. They say that chewing the nuts will kill me. So I said maybe I shouldn't be out walking because I might get hit by a car."

But that didn't sound like a complaint at all. To Chunmu, his friend's smug look was a put-down that irked him, even though he knew that Tianfu was not trying to make him feel bad.

Two or three decades back, Tianfu, who'd had four daughters in a row, was envious of Chunmu for having three sons. One night Tianfu looked him up on the temple grounds to ask him the secret of his success. Chunmu knew he'd had no say in this matter and that it couldn't be accomplished through knowledge or technical skills. Yet Tianfu's guileless look seemed to be asking Chunmu to take advantage of him, so Chunmu demanded a free meal before he'd teach him a technique. Tianfu agreed to everything, and Chunmu kept his promise; when Tianfu said that making that happen with his wife would be hard, Chunmu said to his friend, "Do you think it's that easy to have boys?"

Early the following morning, Tianfu came to see him in the cowshed to whisper what had happened the night before. He had followed Chunmu's instructions, but ended up with cramped thighs, and his wife nearly died of suffocation. Tianfu would have thought he wasn't up to the task if Chunmu hadn't burst out laughing until he doubled over. Tianfu was understandably upset when Chunmu betrayed himself with roaring laughter. Cursing Chunmu for joking about such a serious matter, Tianfu balled up his fists to hit him. Knowing he shouldn't have done that, Chunmu apologized with a threat that people would be laughing at Tianfu and his wife, not him, if they found out. Tianfu relaxed his fists, but he couldn't stop saying that Chunmu would die a terrible death. It didn't take long for all the villagers to learn about what had happened, and even the children, who had only a vague idea what it was all about, laughed behind his back when they saw Tianfu walk by, calling him Cramp Legs.

With three sons, Chunmu did not have to worry about continuing the family line. But times change, and Chunmu's life changed along with them; as his sons grew up and had families of their own, it felt to him as if he had no sons and grandsons. He remained alone in Toufen Village, where he made a living by harvesting bamboo shoots every spring and summer. His wife had died two years earlier, which had more than doubled his workload around the house. It finally dawned on him how much she had been doing. Back when they'd had fights, she would complain about how he thought he was carrying a heavy load by taking care of all the deities, and how he wouldn't lift a finger to help, but would nag her mercilessly. Now he understood why. Their sons, who had made infrequent visits home, all but stopped coming back to Toufen. Chunmu was a reasonable man, and he knew that his sons, all country boys, weren't cut out for running a business. His oldest had apprenticed as an electrician and had become, to put it nicely, his own boss. But without enough capital, he could not bid for major projects and had to beg for small jobs that sometimes even cost him money. The second son managed to eke out a living tending a betel nut stand. It would be unfair to say he wasn't doing okay for himself, since he at least had gotten himself a young Betel Nut Beauty for a wife. One summer when they came back for a visit, Chunmu said that she dressed like a spider demon in *Journey to the West*; they never returned after that. The youngest one, a factory worker, kept changing jobs and could not settle down. Since none of them were doing well, Chunmu had suggested that they all come home. "President

Lee Teng-hui said to focus on sperm-sized agriculture, which is something you young people should know. We have nearly an acre of land, so if you all come back, we can work together." His sons laughed when they finally understood what he was talking about. Chunmu, who did not speak Mandarin, had pronounced "special-sized agriculture" as "sperm-sized." But he wouldn't have known what it was even if he'd known the proper term. All he cared about was that there was still hope for farmers; he didn't mind being laughed at by his sons for his unintelligible Mandarin, as long as he could say a few words to vent his frustration. He gave the matter some thought and said, "*If it's not sperm-sized agriculture, then teach me how to say what it is in Taiwanese. Show me. Come on. Show me how to say it.*" But his sons just laughed, for in fact they would have been hard-pressed to show do that. What was hardest for him, however, was that they agreed they would be laughed at if they came back to work the land. "Laughed at? For working the land? How can I not complain when young people say something like that?" He complained about his sons when people asked about them, as if they were someone else's sons.

He had no idea when his mouth had become independent of him and refused to be reined in. His mouth woke up each morning the moment he opened his eyes at daybreak, and began to chatter away. He grumbled about whatever came into his view. Sometimes, when a chick chirped after falling into a ditch, he would jabber away, even though all he had to do was bend over, fish the chick out, and return it to the hen. Even with years of experience, his wife still could not block out the noise and enjoy a little peace and quiet. "Are you scolding the hen or me, old man?" she would say with a laugh from inside the house.

"So what if I'm talking about you? Do you plan to ask the deities to side with you?" He felt that his mouth had betrayed him. Who would believe him if he said that his mouth, not him, was in control? He would surely be sent to the insane asylum in Songshan if he dared to utter such nonsense. Strangely enough, however, his mouth was well behaved when he was out, a companion to his smiling face. So he ran out and took his mouth with him whenever something like that happened at home; if he didn't, there would be no peace in the house on that day.

On his way home from Tianfu's house, he ran into a villager returning from selling bamboo shoots at the market. "Back already? How was today's price?"

"Bad. It was twenty-eight NT when the wholesalers came to buy early in the morning, and it dropped to fifteen just before I came home. The people from Zhentou, Neicheng-zai, and Sancheng all came to sell theirs in our market. There's too much work waiting for me at home, so I had to sell, even for fifteen."

"I had to be at Tianfu's house this morning, so I asked Shuiji to sell mine for me."

"He's still there. I asked him to come back with me, but he said he'd stay till the evening, since he has nothing to do at home. How was the funeral? Pretty impressive, I imagine."

"Of course. All the monks and nuns and Taoist priests were there reciting sutras and chants. Lots of people went to pay their respects."

"With his filial daughters and successful sons-in-law, they could put on as big a funeral as they want."

Chunmu clammed up at the mention of filial, successful children. He walked off and stopped at the intersection, where he righted a sign pointing to the Three Deities Temple, complaining first about how the sign refused to stand up straight and then the despicable passerby who had knocked it over. Why did he have to do that? Wasn't he afraid the gods would take off his hand?

Over the previous New Year's holiday, he had followed the village clerk's suggestion to make more than thirty signs for the Three Deities Temple, hoping to attract farmers from all over Taiwan to stop and visit as their tour buses took them to worship at temples around the island. Chunmu had found someone to write the signs and treated the man to a meal, but they weren't done until the summer. He then planted them all the way from the exit off the No. 9 Highway to the Three Deities Temple, yet they managed to draw only three tour groups in a year.

The first group, from Manzhou in Pingdong, came in a large tour bus on the third day the signs were up. Chunmu had been so impressed by the clerk that he wished he could put the man on the altar and make him the twenty-eighth Buddha. He was upset that the signs hadn't been up during New Year's; otherwise, who knew what would have—. But he had no time to worry about that, because the pilgrims had arrived. They got off the bus and stood to the left of the temple, asking where the Three Deities Temple was. They all did a double take and stared at each other after Chunmu pointed at the ordinary-looking structure next to them, which was made of corrugated metal, like a private house. He was annoyed when they laughed, as if they were under the influence of a laughing spell.

"Don't just stand here laughing. Go on in and see the twenty-seven deities."

Three or four of the pilgrims had gone inside after getting off the bus, but it was too hot, hotter than outside, so hot that even the deities' beards had curled up. Some of those still outside followed Chunmu in. He turned the ceiling fan to the highest speed, making it shake and groan like a servant gasping for breath to prove himself to his master. The pilgrims were frightened when they looked up at the fan, which was more like a helicopter spiraling down on them.

"Oh, no! The fan is going to fall," someone said.

"It won't. Trust me. It's always been like that," Chunmu said, but despite his reassurance, he turned the speed down to the lowest setting before following the visitors out. He could not hold their attention to tell them about each of the deities because they were all looking for a toilet and some water.

"Over there, next door. You can use the toilet in my house," Chunmu offered eagerly.

Following his direction, they skirted a myrtle fence and stormed into Chunmu's house. Some stood in line, some rested in his living room, while a few went looking for water in the kitchen. They were now guests in his house, he told himself cheerfully, as he hustled in and out, busily making them feel at home.

"You men who just want to pee can go out into the bamboo grove."

"Would you like some of those? If so, you can have them cheap." He made a sales pitch when he spotted seven or eight unsold bamboo shoots under the eave. "They aren't too heavy to take on the bus. Bamboo shoots from Toufen are sweet and tender, like pears. The most famous in Taiwan—"

"Right. Well known in Dinggang and famous in Xiagang." A vivacious female pilgrim cut him off. "Would *you* like some? If so, you can have them for nothing when you visit us in Manzhou. How's that?"

The tourists laughed at her retort. Chunmu had to agree with her. They were from the countryside, with their own bamboo groves and plenty of shoots. "You're right." He laughed along with them.

The tour bus made a thunderous roar as the driver pressed the gas pedal. Someone came in and said, "The bus can't turn around."

"Be careful! Don't knock over my temple," Chunmu shouted as he ran out, drawing another round of laughter from the visitors.

The visitors left. The visit had not been a total failure. Five of the women had bought candles and incense and he had managed to collect three hundred NT in alms. He could have done better, but it was a good beginning.

He went inside the temple, lit three sticks of incense, and stood before the sacrificial table to mutter to the deities. "*Now, that's the way to go. Me alone offering incense isn't going to be enough. We have to get all of the pilgrims to do it.*" Chunmu thought he had hit upon something clever when he said all of them. *Yes, that's right. This is the Three Deities Temple, and all deities need all pilgrims to prosper. We won't compete with Mazu in Beigang or Enzhugong in Taipei, but we have to do better than the Erjie Protector or the Buddha Temple at Qingshuigou. Don't you think? I'm not greedy, but you have to consider my situation. I'm going broke just offering you incense, candles, and tea. How many years has it been now? I've served you for almost thirty years. You all know I consider myself lucky if my sons don't come to me for money. I would never think of counting on them. So this is what you need to do. Bring more pilgrims like today, protect my health, help those worthless sons of mine stay healthy and make big money, and make sure their sons are good students.*"

Chunmu had noticed that the once lush grass by the temple was a mess, but he'd been too busy letting his mouth grumble to tend to it. When he came out again after taking care of the temple, he saw that the bus had churned the grass up as it tried to back out, as if two bulls had been fighting. "People these days are so careless," he complained. "It wasn't all that far, so why couldn't they have just walked in? The space here is so small. Why did the bus have to drive in? It could have parked at the intersection." But he realized that he shouldn't have blamed the bus driver when he recalled the last road sign. He had placed it at the intersection pointing inside, and of course the driver had followed it. It was his fault; he hadn't been thinking clearly. Speaking of thinking clearly, he looked down to check his fly before dragging his feet back and forth to smooth the furrowed ground, only to break the toe straps on his plastic sandals. "Didn't I tell you it wouldn't work? See, you've ruined your sandals. Go back inside and get a hoe. That's the way to do it." But once he was inside, where the table and chairs were scattered about, he forgot what he had come in to do. He walked into the toilet. "Did those men have forked peckers?" he shouted. "How did they get it all over the floor? All of them, not just a couple. What a disgusting bunch. This is what people mean when they say a hen that won't lay eggs leaves chicken shit everywhere."

He walked outside and looked into the sky. "There's the sky up there, killing us with its blistering sun. Why doesn't it send down some rain?" That's how his mouth worked, nagging, griping, and grousing all day long. His complaints were like scattered bullets, some of which even hit the sky.

More than a month went by before the second tour group showed up. He had decided not to offer them any tea or water. The first two of the six tour buses from Fanlu, Jiayi, turned onto the path, where the drivers' view was blocked by the overgrown branches of some wax apple trees. They backed out for fear of scratching their buses or hearing complaints from the tree owners. The path was too narrow for them, and even the seasoned drivers had a hard time backing out because of the branches. Chunmu felt sorry for them. He had wanted to remove the sign after the first tour, but had forgotten. As the drivers struggled, Chunmu led the tour leader to the temple.

"You can park on the main road. It only takes seven or eight minutes to walk over."

"What deities do you worship here?"

"All of them. One visit here will save you from visiting other temples." Chunmu continued when he saw the confused look on the man's face. "I have twenty-seven deities here. That includes Ji Gong, the Crazy Monk, if you need numbers for the lottery."

The temple came into view after they walked past an old camphor tree.

"This is it?" The tour leader couldn't believe his eyes. "This is the place?" He needed confirmation.

Chunmu was about to say yes, but stopped when he saw the disbelief on the man's face.

"Your signs are bigger than your temple!" Refusing to even walk to the entrance, the guide turned and walked away, waving his hands and shaking his head.

Chunmu was left standing there, feeling offended, puzzled by the man's comment. He looked at the guide's receding back. "He didn't even go inside to take a look before saying—" Chunmi stopped, knowing it was pointless to complain. But his mouth would not give up. "What did he know? I have more deities than anyone but the shops that carve statues. I dare him to name a temple with more deities than mine anywhere on the island.

Sure, the shops have more, but they need to be gilded, have the eyes opened, and be installed on a sacrificial table. They're just wooden figurines. You can't call them deities. He knows nothing, and yet he had the nerve to spew nonsense. What did he mean? The signs are bigger than the temple? How could he say such insulting things about the deities?" He turned to look at the humiliated temple, which stood there looking innocent, its door resembling a gaping, silent mouth. By the time he reached the intersection, he saw the tail end of the last bus before it turned and disappeared. A few villagers were standing by the shops at the intersection, watching the buses leave.

"What? They just left like that?" They knew what had happened, but asked anyway.

"Yes, they left," he said offhandedly.

"Did they burn any incense?"

"No, they didn't." Chunmu smiled awkwardly.

"What a shame. They were right outside the door."

"What can you do? You can't force their feet to walk in."

Chunmu did not want to hang around, though the villagers were eager to talk. He turned and left, and even after he had walked a ways down the path, he could still hear them talking about him; in his ears, their comments seemed ambivalent and insinuating. The sympathetic ones felt sorry for him, while the scornful ones thought he was in over his head. The lively branches of the wax apple trees reached across the path, as if in greeting, but they were suspended in midair, like outstretched hands, unable to decide if they should pull back as he walked on looking dispirited.

Chunmu did his best to calm the turmoil inside. It was fine that they didn't get off to the buses to burn incense. *There were so many of them.* He did a quick calculation and came up with about two hundred altogether. *They'd have torn down the temple if they all came in, and flooded it if they'd used the toilet in the house. That wouldn't have worked. Besides, I don't have a huge supply of candles and incense.* He felt better after going through various scenarios, all of them dealing with the impossibility of handling so many visitors, as if he had been lucky to avoid a disaster. But no sooner was he feeling calmer than his mind was roiled again by different thoughts. *So many people, and just imagine if each one offered even a hundred NT. A hundred isn't too much. I've been to temples where I offered at least two hundred. One hundred is a low figure; some might even give a thousand or more. But in any case, how much would it be if they all offered a hundred NT?* Unable to get over the missed opportunity, he patted his chest, his heart knotted with regret.

His mind wandered, and for some reason he recalled a childhood visit to his mother's older brother at Dakenggu. He'd gone to the beach to watch his uncle and others catch fish with a net. His uncle was yelling at the men, "Let go, let go. The net's about to rip. Let it go, right now." Everyone heard his panicky shout and dropped the net they were dragging closer to shore, sending all the fish, big and small, back into the ocean. It would have torn from the weight if they had dragged it ashore; they would have would up with no fish and destroyed the tool of their livelihood in the process. It would have been a disaster. The men who would have been paid from that day's catch all looked downcast, while saying that it was the right thing to do. *What's yours will be yours, no matter what, and what you don't get is never intended for you anyway. It's as simple as that.* He tried to console himself, but a few days later he was still thinking how he could get the tourists, the metaphorical hens, to stick around and lay eggs, if another six buses showed up. It was no easy task, and in the end he had to say to himself, *It's like a flea eating croton seeds. Don't take a laxative if you don't have a bunghole.*

The third group consisted of a family of four who had driven over on their own. Not typical pilgrims who traveled to all the temples on the island, the couple were white-collar workers from Taipei, taking advantage of a free weekend to visit Yilan. The signs on the No. 9 Highway had piqued their curiosity enough that they drove by to see the temple. Chunmu had just come back from fertilizing the bamboo when he saw people walking out of the temple.

"Are you here to burn incense?" he asked with a big smile.

"We're just looking around." The husband was holding a young child.

"Come, come offer your respects. The deities will protect you and help you make big money." Chunmu did his best to delay them a while longer.

"We did that already. We've been here for quite some time." The man continued, "Who are the deities?"

"What do you do for a living? There's Ji Gong, if you want a number for the lottery—" Chunmu stopped when the young woman laughed. He didn't think he'd said anything funny, so what was she laughing about? Was he being funny? He was perplexed when the husband smiled and said, "I'm a teacher."

So? What was so funny? Chunmu was even more puzzled now. But he was not the type who needed to get to the bottom of things, so he followed up on the man's answer and offered, "I've got one for you, too. The Deity for Literary Studies, best for teachers and students."

"Why have you prepared so many of them here?"

"What?" Chunmu was confused. "What do you mean by 'prepare'?" He needed time to understand how a deity could be prepared.

"What I mean is, what do you expect from having so many deities?"

Chunmu thought he knew what the man wanted, so he said, "Do you want to know how I ended up installing so many deities? Ah, that's a long story."

They picked a shady spot under the old banyan tree and sat down on a couple of large rocks to talk. The professor was an academic, so he showed great interest in the origin and development of the temple. He took notes and pictures. Chunmu, who thought the story might appear in newspapers to advertise for his temple, was eager to share everything he knew; he and his mouth worked in unison, leaving no question unanswered and throwing in extra information whenever they could.

His family had had only one son for each of several generations, starting with his great-grandfather, Xie Cheng, to his grandfather, Xie Yingchuan, to his father, Xie Wangquan, and to him, Xie Chunmu. Chunmu in particular had been frail and sickly before he got married, like a candle in the wind. Everyone in the Xie clan, including married women who were taking care of others' families, was worried sick about the Xie family line. Whenever he showed any sign of a health problem, everyone sprang into action, seeking divination with the deities, sending for a doctor, and following instructions from itinerant practitioners of quack medicine. Sometimes the women would get a folk formula and offer it to him. One of them was more like a medication for cattle, with more than seventy ingredients. He had taken too much medicine and suffered countless times, but he felt a sense of pride when he related the terrible experience now.

"How did I take the medicine? They had to force the liquid down my throat. One would hold my head, others grabbed my hands and feet, while another pinched my nose. I couldn't break free no matter how hard I fought. I'd moan and wail even before they started, even worse when they got down to work. When the neighbors heard me screech, they said we were slaughtering pigs at our house again." Chunmu laughed, amused by his own accounts.

The professor was beginning to fidget. After talking all this time, Chunmu had yet to mention the temple. Obviously, it would be a while before they got to that. The older child, a first-grader, was squirming by his mother, clearly eager to leave. The man turned to look at his son and smiled.

"Let's go," his wife murmured in English.

"No. Sorry. This is a wonderful case," the husband replied in English.

"What's wrong?" Chunmu asked, afraid that they'd get up and leave.

"Nothing. The boy is being a pest."

"Come, Grandpa will show you something."

"Go on, go see it with Grandpa."

A whispered argument arose after Chunmu walked off with the child.

"He never shuts up. How long are we going to stay here and listen to his story?"

"Haven't you learned anything from my classes? We're doing fieldwork here. Country folks generally have no sense of time, and their stories tend to be jumbled. What we want is tied up in his long-winded tale, and there's nothing an interviewer can do. You can't edit and write up the research in the middle of the interview, and you won't get anything if you expect him to answer only your questions."

"I don't want any more lessons. I'd still be your live-in maid no matter how much I've learned."

"Stop that nonsense."

"Can't you come back some other time?"

"It's good timing! You know that," he replied in English again.

Chunmu was back with the child, who looked thrilled, riding a tricycle made of wood, possibly the only one in the world. The couple was tickled at the silly look of the bike.

"I made this for my grandson. They don't live here, and no one rides it."

The earlier discord between the husband and wife was replaced by cheerfulness when they saw their child ride up, laughing and shouting, to show them the cute vehicle. They praised Chunmu's handiwork; he added with pride that he could make many other things, opening up a new topic in their conversation. The professor interrupted at the right moment: "Where did the Three Deities Temple come from? Who set it up, with whose money? How did it become what it is today?"

"Oh, that's a long story."

The response made the couple groan inwardly, but outwardly they smiled and encouraged him to go on.

As he gazed off into the distance, Chunmu returned to many years earlier. Each deity, he told them, had been invited into his house to take command and ensure peace or for his family to receive a medicinal formula each time he had a serious illness. Sometimes he was even offered up to be adopted by the deities.

"Did the deities all agree to adopt you?"

"That's easy to find out," Chunmu said with a smile. "They can't talk, nor can they nod or shake their heads. So we talked to them and cast a pair of divination pieces. If one of them didn't agree, we just kept casting the pieces, and sooner or later we'd get the result we wanted."

"Can you do that?" The professor was perplexed.

"Why not? For instance, my family asked a deity if he would adopt me. If they got one piece facing up and one down, it meant the deities agreed. If both were facing up, the so-called smiley sign, it meant he thought it was funny and we could cast again. When both were facing down, the covered sign, it meant he refused. But we could always change our question or ask if it hadn't been stated clearly and repeat the question before casting again. If you kept at it, you'd naturally get the consenting sign. And you could always get someone else to cast the divination if you kept getting the answer you didn't want."

"But isn't that like tricking the deities?" The professor laughed.

"'Trick' is not a nice word. That's just the way we ask the deities and Buddha for help." Chunmu added, "You'll know how many major illnesses I suffered by counting the number of deities in the temple, not mentioning minor problems, which weren't included."

"Did you stop getting sick later?"

"I know it sounds weird, but I didn't seem to have any major problem after I got married." He laughed. "And the Xie family finally has three sons in my generation. We could have had more if my wife hadn't fallen and miscarried when she was out getting water."

"Hormones," the professor turned to say to his wife with a smile, afraid that she was getting bored.

"Right. Horumon. That's what some people said." Chunmu

repeated the word in Japanese style.

"You're quite something, Ojisan. You knew the English word I used."

"English? I know only 'ABC, dog bites piggy.'" Chunmu was reminded of a children's ditty from years ago. "You hear it in TV ads all the time. Oh, and guys like me joke about horumon all the time, too."

He digressed again, this time about how he had finally decided on Chunmu after changing his name several times, following the suggestion of an old monk who had come for alms. The monk mentioned something like "A withering tree sprouts again when spring comes" and "Sun-facing flowers and trees meet spring early." So he settled on chun, spring, and mu, trees. His health greatly improved after the birth of his third son, but it was hard to say exactly why, except that the twenty-seven deities had played a role, with the help of the name change, the secret formulae offered by the Xie women, and his wife's hormones.

The births of three boys, a significant development, made the whole Xie clan, past and present, breathe a collective sigh of relief. But after all these years, Chunmu often looked deflated when the subject of his sons came up, a stark contrast to the time of his first son's birth. Back then the baby had given Chunmu a great deal of face in the Xie clan, which had so few males. They had been dirt-poor, but they knew they had to show their gratitude to the deities. A whole pig had been out of their reach. They had thought about using the rice sprouts to get a high-interest loan, but unfortunately the Lanyang area had suffered three years of floods. After exhausting all their means, they eventually decided they could buy a pig's head and a pig's tail, a symbolic pig, to repay the deities. But his aunt objected, telling them that they must not break their promise to the deities. She said everyone could chip in and they could buy a smaller pig; the deities would understand that the poor could not afford to offer them a hog.

"Their compassion is how they became deities, but we must be true to our word, too." Spurred by his aunt, the other female relatives offered either cash or their gold rings, pooling enough money to buy a small pig, which, as the runt of a litter, never even reached a hundred kilos. The size notwithstanding, they were able to slaughter a pig to offer to the deities and keep their promise. They heard some unkind words from mean-spirited villagers about how the pig Xie Wangquan slaughtered was more like a skinny goat. That was still better than being laughed at for trying to pass off a pig's head and tail for a whole pig. A whole pig remained out of their reach when Chunmu had the second and the third sons. Lucky for them, since they hadn't promised a pig either time. What they had offered instead was to give every one of the dozens of families in the village steamed sticky rice and a red-dyed egg. With generations of the Xie family praying for a son, who would have imagined Chunmu sighing at the mention of his boys?

"Let's not talk about them."

"You're very fortunate to have three sons." The professor tried to make him feel better.

"Good fortune? More like good-for-nothing fortune."

The professor promised to come back, but they never did. He left a business card, and Chunmu put it next to his ID card in his wallet and took it out as proof when he told people about his friend, a college professor with a Ph.D. No one else came, either, but Chunmu's memory was hazy.

After returning from Tianfu's funeral, Chunmu went straight

to the temple, where he stood outside the door and put his hands together to offer his respect to the deities inside. The phone rang when he was about to walk in and tell the deities what had happened that day, as he did every day, which would be about Tianfu's memorial, his daughters, and Chunmu's own sons. It had been ringing for quite some time, but he had been too lost in thought to notice. He raced home, but it stopped ringing the moment he picked it up. He received so few calls that he always felt he'd missed something important when he did not get to the phone in time. His mouth started up again, nagging him nonstop. The same thing had happened twice recently. He'd skirted the fence and run into the house, but just as he reached for the phone, it picked that moment to stop ringing. To make excuses so his mouth would not blame him, he'd say the caller had little patience. Each time he missed a call, he would think about making an opening in the fence so he could walk straight from the temple into his house. But it was only a fleeting thought, and though he did talk about it often, he never actually picked up a hoe to dig up a few of the bushes. That had gone on for a long time, and now the crape myrtles were nearly the size of a tallow tree. He was getting old and useless; all he had left was his mouth. Pacing by the phone, Chunmu mumbled about himself when it rang again. He picked it up after the first ring.

"Who's this?" Chunmu barked.

"It's me, Xie Shenglong," the caller barked back.

"Who do you want?" Chunmu shouted, thrown off by the familiar and yet strange-sounding name.

"Ah-pa, it's me, Ah-long. Wang-zai said you gave him the deed to get a mortgage from a bank—" Ah-long was the son who tended a betel nut stand. He sounded anxious and harried, but

Chunmu would not let him finish, puzzled and incensed over the willful, formal tone his son had used in giving his name.

"What did you say? Shay what?" Chunmu pretended not to have misheard. "What kind of chickenshit name is that? You don't show any respect when you talk to your old man. What was your name again?" What really irked him was that he could hear his daughter-in-law, the spider demon, whispering nearby, telling his son what to say to his own father.

Despite the blowup, Chunmu got a pretty good sense of what was going on. Ah-long had gotten a call from the oldest son, Shengwang, who said their father had agreed to let him mortgage the land for two million NT to start an electrical business in China with a partner. It had prompted Ah-long to call his father, but no one had answered the phone all morning, which had gotten him wondering. And the more he had thought about it, the more upset he was; how could their father make such an important decision without talking with them? Ah-long added that he would be coming home that afternoon.

"Don't come home. I'm not here."

He had barely put the phone down when it rang again. He did not want to pick it up, but the handset seemed to have taken control of his hand.

"You're a hard man to find, Ah-pa. I've been calling all morning. I finally got through, but then you were on the phone. Who were you talking to? It went on forever." Number three son sounded equally ruffled.

"What's gotten into you and your brother today? Raising hell! Ah-long just finished arguing with me, and now it's your turn. What do you want? Haven't I done enough for you?" Chunmu could not bring himself to be nice.

"Ah-pa, I'm Ah-fa, not Wang-zai."

Ah-fa was calling about the same thing, with the intention of stopping their father. If Chunmu had not been burning with anger, he would have died from the chill he felt when he learned that his three sons were fighting over his land with their own plans in mind while he was still alive. Ah-fa said he would be coming back with Ah-long.

Chunmu was so outraged that he promised himself not to answer their calls. But the phone rang again the moment he put it down, nearly making him jump. "Don't get it," he told himself. "I'm getting it," he snapped at the phone on the third ring. "Hello?" The handset made it up to his ear by the fifth ring.

"It's me, Ah-pa. Wang-zai." His oldest was less confrontational.

Wang-zai's tone made it hard for Chunmu to scream at him. But he was still fuming from the first two calls, which had actually been caused by Wang-zai, so he could not be patient with his son even though he did try to control his temper. "What do you want?"

"Don't go out this afternoon. I'm coming back to see you."

"What is this? A fox guarding a henhouse? I know you want to talk to me about the land. I don't want to talk about it, and you don't have to come back."

"Eh, did Ah-long and Ah-fa say something to you?"

"Who else could it be? A ghost?"

"It's not like that."

"Oh, what is it like, then?"

"It's too complicated to explain over the phone. Wait till this afternoon; we'll talk about it this afternoon. I'm bringing my son with me. The older one is at school, and I'll bring the younger back to see you." Wang-zai had married late, so he had young children.

"No, you'd better not."

Yet his mind got busy. It would take them only a couple of hours to return from Taipei; he went to his tool shed and found the wooden tricycle and a rocking horse. He cleared the spider webs and wiped off the dust, cheered by the image of his grandson riding them. His good mood was dampened by an embarrassing thought—was the younger grandson called Xie Yingcai or Xie Deqin? He blamed old age and a bad memory, but he was unhappy with his son, too. Why had he waited so long to bring the grandsons back to see him? Chunmu went into the house, where he rummaged through a desk drawer and found the notebook recording predictions of the two grandsons' future done by a fortuneteller a few years back. He learned that the younger one's name was Yingcai. As he read on, he saw "Beware of water in the year of ren-wu." This was the year of ren-wu, so the child must stay clear of water. Chunmu congratulated himself on opening it right to that page, and reminded himself to alert his son to the warning. Despite his anticipation at seeing his grandson, his mind was thrown into turmoil again when he thought about the issue with the land. He was upset but fearful. Each of his three sons had his own designs on the family property, something he had been aware of all along, but it would soon become a real headache. He had no idea what to do. Aimlessly he walked to the kitchen, then to the pigless pigpen out back, and to the tool shed on the other side before returning to the front of the house. After doing that a time or two, he thought he knew what to do; he skirted the fence and went into the temple, where he gazed helplessly at the deities. Once the solemn expressions on their faces managed to calm him down and give him some peace, he lit three sticks of incense and offered his respects in front of the central incense burner. With the incense sticks held piously to his chest, he squinted through the smoke, tilted his head slightly, and murmured,

All you deities,
Your adopted son, Xie Chunmu, is here to ask piously
To plead with you
To protect my three sons.
Please ensure that Wang-zai, Ah-long, and Ah-fa are healthy and make big money
Don't let them try all day long
To get their hands on the ancestral property
Isn't it just like all the stars with you up there in the sky
That must be well taken care of?
All you deities,
Your adopted son, Xie Chunmu, is here to ask piously
To plead with you
Please protect the Xie family and let no harm come to anyone
Have you heard me, all you deities?
All you deities, I—

He was keenly aware of how insignificant, weak, and fragile he was as he made a helpless but pious plea to the omnipotent deities. The incense smoke made his eyes water, and despite repeated deep breaths, his body shuddered and constricted, as if the all-seeing deities had passed right through him. It was over in an instant. Gone was his fear of facing his sons and dealing with their fight over the property; Chunmu now felt he was ready for their visit.

After sticking the incense properly in the burner, he took a step back to bow one more time, and his independent mouth woke up. There by the sacrificial table, it complained, as before, about the deities for not doing their job, as if talking to old friends. *Let's not even talk about my father and his father, it said, and just focus on me. Since I became the head of the Xie family, I've offered my respects and service to you for over thirty years, without missing a day. It's been trying, even if you don't consider it much of a contribution. Don't get me wrong; I'm filled with gratitude for your protection and for giving me three sons. But you did nott help me raise them.* Chunmu looked over at Guan Gong, the Warrior God, and continued: *Aren't you the one promoting loyalty and the code of honor? I can't get a hint of loyalty, filial piety, benevolence, or sense of brotherhood from any of the three boys. We can forget everything else, but what about filial piety? Not a shred of it! Tell me, does that make sense to you?* Bolstered by a sense of injustice from his friends, Chunmu was talking up a storm. A redheaded fly flitted in and landed on the tip of the Earth God's nose, close to where he was standing. Chunmu reached out to chase it away, but it kept returning to the same spot. *Earth God*, Chunmu moved on, *you know very well where my bamboo grove is, don't you? In recent days, insects have been taking big bites out of the shoots, especially the large, meaty ones. No one would will bamboo shoots like those at the market; I couldn't give them away. What do I have to do to get you to chase the bugs away? I offer you tea and incense three hundred and sixty-five days a year; I may not do it at the same time every day, but I never miss a day. I always do my best by offering three meat dishes and liquor over New Year's and other holidays. I'm not saying you have to repay me, but look at it from my perspective. After years of service and reverence, I deserve your help even if I wasn't your adopted son. But you did adopt me. When the students take their exams, I see on the TV news how so many mothers take their children to worship at the Temple of Literary*

Studies they've just about worn down the doorsill. So why don't you bring some students to worship here. It's for your sake, not mine. Think about it. This place, with its tin roof, is bone-chilling cold in the winter and stifling hot in the summer. Doesn't the cold or the heat bother you? Have you ever thought about living in a better temple? It would look so much better to have a nicer temple. I've been thinking about it on your behalf. It costs money. You can't do anything without money. But where are we going to get money if we don't have any pilgrim tours coming to worship, if no one shows up at your door? Everyone says the deities have divine power, so all you twenty-seven deities—Chunmu hit upon an idea—*all you twenty-seven deities display your divine power by appearing in the dreams of tour leaders all over the island and instruct them to come worship here. You have to show yourselves. The small size of our Three Deities Temple isn't a problem as long as we have you and your divine power. If you could pull that off, everyone would come to Toufen; they'd even make the climb if we were on a snowy mountaintop. Why do you think some of the temples see so many worshipers? That's because the deities show up in people's dreams and display their divine power.*

Chunmu was feeling better now. He could carp at the deities, and none of his sons could take that from him. Exhilarated by letting his complaints flow so freely, he showed no sign of letting up, even though the three sticks of incense had burning down. *Do you know that my sons are now fighting over the ancestral land? Your temple is situated right on the land, so you and I will be homeless if they have their way with it.* He took a deep breath and continued: *I don't mind being homeless, but I'll bet you'd have trouble dealing with it.* Chunmu's attention was drawn to the fly on the Earth God's nose, where it was scratching its head and rubbing its wings. He was distracted enough to notice the Earth God's face, which had been carved in such way that it seemed to be laughing and crying at the same time. He changed the subject. *Why are you laughing? I'm telling the truth.* When he ran into problems, he either brought the deities to his level and treated them like old friends, or placed them on a pedestal so he could pray and beg for their help. They were there to listen to his complaints, his grumbling, even his reproaches. He had something new on this day—his sons' fight over the ancestral land and his fear that it could be lost. In the past he'd often said to others how times were changing; now he finally understood what that meant.

Back inside the phone was ringing, bringing his talk with the deities to an abrupt end as he raced around the fence to answer it. He was panting hard.

"Wait, wait a minute. Let—let me catch my breath."

"Hello? Is this the San Jose Motel?" Click! Chunmu was so frustrated, he slammed down the phone and cursed, "Fuck your grandmother! What a fool. Mistaking the police station for a whorehouse? You nearly killed me."

It had all started a couple of months ago. He kept getting calls looking for the motel. Once he was so fed up he told the caller he'd called a coffin shop. Pissed, the caller began harassing him by calling every day, and sometimes late at night. He had been distressed each time the phone rang because he could not decide whether to answer it or not. Now he was on edge over the phone because he didn't want to miss calls from his sons, who had not been in touch often but were coming home on this day.

Drawn away from the temple by a wrong number, he did not know what to do next. He paced and puttered around. His heart nearly stopped when he walked into the kitchen and spotted a cleaver. *Ai-yo! I have to put that away.* It would be horrible if that damned Ah-long, with all his tattoos of dragons and tigers, got into a fight with his brothers over the land and picked that up It had already happened a couple of times with him. In addition to the cleaver, Chunmu also hid an axe, a pair of fire tongs, and other tools under his bed. The new worry dogged him, like a playful fly following a scabby head, and he had trouble concentrating. Somehow he found his way back to the temple, where he lit another three sticks of incense and raised his head to pray:

All you deities,
Your adopted son, Xie Chunmu, is here to ask piously
To plead with you
To ensure that the boys will be nice to each other when they're here
Don't let them fight
Your adopted son, Xie Chunmu, is here to ask piously
To plead with you

After putting the incense in the burner, he was about to step out when he turned his head and stopped be side the table. He faced the deities and said in a worried voice, "Did you hear what I asked just now, all you deities? My second son, the one selling betel nuts, is the most difficult one. You must keep an eye on him and make sure he doesn't cause trouble. Guan Gong, you know martial arts, so you're in charge of him. We'll talk about worshipers later, deities. Just make sure they don't get in a fight. Did you hear me?"

Chunmu ambled down the path to the intersection with the main road. His sons would not arrive for a while yet, but he did not know what to do to fill the time. He would not know and would not confirm, if someone were to ask if he'd come to the intersection to wait for them. A tour bus had parked by one end of the nearby bridge to change a tire. He'd heard it was an island tour for residents of a nursing home down south. The old folks had gotten out of the bus; some were walking around, while about a dozen of them sat silent and unmoving on the cement railings. Chunmu was taken aback by one of them, a familiar face that looked like a beardless Kaizhang Shengwang, General Chen, who had brought peace to Zhangzhou, the ancestral city of many Taiwanese. He looked over at the others. How strange: they all bore a resemblance to the deities in his temple! There were the Earth God, Ji Gong the Crazy Monk, Lü Dongbing, one of the famed eight immortals, Niupuza the Heavenly King, and so on. He felt like going up to chat with them, but now he stood still and gazed at the railing. The old men sitting there had been looking at different things, but their curiosity was piqued when they noticed someone gazing at them with surprise written on his face. With all of them now turned in his direction, Chunmu noticed more familiar faces, Patriarch Qingshui and the King of Five Grains, who tasted a hundred herbs. Seized by an unfamiliar panic, Chunmu turned to leave, but he looked down and saw the driver's sweaty baby face. The driver looked up at him, and ai! Wasn't that Nezha, the Rebel Third Prince?

His heart racing, Chunmu followed the path, feigning calm strides, though he knew he was walking strangely. *What a coincidence. But is it really? It might be if only one or two of them looked like deities, but all of them? That can't be a coincidence,* Chunmu said fearfully to himself as he walked on. *All you deities. You've got me wrong. My mouth talked trash, but it meant nothing bad. Honestly, I have no bad intentions. I swear. If I, Xie Chunmu, harbor any ill intentions, let lightning strike me down and take away all my children and grandchildren.*

The Three Deities Temple came into view when he made a turn at the camphor tree. He strode over and put his hands together to bow, before walking inside to light three sticks of incense. With all the piety he could muster, he looked up at the deities, then changed his mind and took a step back to kneel:

All you deities,
Your adopted son, Xie Chunmu, is here to ask piously
To plead with you

2002

Variations on a Canary's Lament

My daughter, Wuyu—Wordless—was seven years old. Autistic and suffering from asthma, she was frail and sickly; her doctor said she had a weak heart and lungs.

It was so sad. At the onset of each cold, dank winter, her friends—her favorite animals, big and small—went into hiding to hibernate, while she had to sit on a tilted bed, tearfully fighting for air. The sight pained my wife so much she shed secret tears; her eyes looked like red dragonflies in winter. All I could do was spend a good part of the night outside by the river, smoking and sighing for some relief. Sometimes I saw shooting stars stray across the evening sky, but I never caught one on which I could pin my urgent, earnest hopes.

That was why I was always grateful when spring arrived. Wuyu could finally lie down to sleep. The simplest action for most people would send my wife tiptoeing from Wuyu's room to my study, where she'd hug me joyfully, holding back happy tears to tell me that our daughter was asleep.

"Let me go take a look," I said on this day, and slipped into her room like a cat. Wuyu was indeed asleep. *She looks absolutely adorable; this is my daughter, Wuyu,* I told myself with a sense of pride. Like Sleeping Beauty in the Disney films. I walked out to get my camera, only to receive a stern look from my wife, who was obviously afraid I'd wake the girl.

I bought a canary for Wuyu one day. Like an autistic child, the canary stays quiet all winter long, and yet it knows spring is here before anyone else. It sings cheerfully when spring is ready to slide down from the hills. Wuyu loved that bird. Whenever it sang, she smiled, like a blooming little flower, and pressed up against the cage. The canary enthralled her, as if she wished she could turn into a bird and climb into the cage.

I was also grateful for the arrival of spring, because my wife's eyes were no longer red and she was back to normal. And I could stop going out to smoke in the cold night wind.

One morning on our day off, my wife and I were startled awake by crisp, melodious sounds. We found that Wuyu had gotten up early to let the bird out. The canary was singing atop a lampshade while Wuyu, standing on a chair, was laughing, reaching up with her head and arms. Dressed in a thin robe, she looked like an angel, lacking only a pair of wings, with the slanting sunlight gathered on her as if by divine intervention.

"Let's not disturb her. She looks so beautiful," I whispered to my wife as we peered at the girl from behind the door.

"That's no good," she said, and went in to get a jacket. "Beautiful won't stop her from catching cold." She went in and put the jacket on our daughter.

She often scolded or glared at me because of Wuyu; we usually focused on different aspects when dealing with the same issue. When it came to Wuyu, she was normally the one with better sense; I considered myself to be sentimental; she preferred the term "foolish."

Wuyu was more stubborn than anyone when she fell in love with an object or had her eye on something. I could do little to help, because she did not talk. But I knew enough to ask her softly from behind when she fixed her gaze on the bird, "You'd like to be a canary, wouldn't you, Wuyu?"

She turned to look at me, intimating the unspoken sentiment on her mind: "Papa, I really do want to be a canary. Can I, Papa?"

"To be a canary." I was saddened by her wish. But then again, why did she have to be who she was now in order to be happy and healthy?

"Yes, but you have to be a singing canary, free of asthma, Wuyu."

Naturally I was hoping she would call me Papa one day, a wish that ought to be easier to grant than her becoming a canary. I told my wife. She laughed at me. "You writers are always getting ideas."

Spring was wonderful, but unpredictable, with its erratic changes in temperature. One night a sudden drop in temperature brought a noise to Wuyu's breathing, like the sound of a broken bellows, a warning to us. It was past her bedtime, but she refused to part with the canary. An autistic child is impossible to deal with once her stubborn nature takes hold, and trying to have it our way would have been very unpleasant. She would have had a fit, or her asthma would have acted up from the agitation and she would have had trouble breathing. My wife and I did our best to talk her into going to bed, but nothing worked. I signaled my weary wife to get some rest. I'd wait until Wuyu began to nod off and carry her to bed.

When she finally looked sleepy, I repeated what I'd said earlier, gently and slowly so as not to upset her. "Listen to Papa, Wuyu. It's late, and the canary needs to sleep. If it doesn't, it won't be able to sing tomorrow, and its yellow feathers will turn black. Papa and Mama need to sleep, and so does the lamp."

She slid off her chair before I finished and went to look at the darkness outside, resting her arms on the windowsill. That was a sign that she was at least willing to leave the cage and let the bird rest. Hanging the cage back up, I said to the canary, "Say thank you to Wuyu, little bird. She wants to let you sleep, and she'll be going to bed soon herself. Make sure you sing to thank her in the morning." I draped a cloth over the cage as I finished.

I could see Wuyu's back as she sprawled on the sill, a sight that reminded me of a Christmas card from overseas: a little girl at a windowsill, gazing at the snow outside with her hands under her chin, waiting for Santa Claus. All Wuyu could see now was an indigo sky dotted with a few stars.

"A shooting star!" I said as one arced across the sky. "Did you see the shooting star, Wuyu?" She looked in the direction of the star. "Did you make a wish, Wuyu? When you see a shooting star, you have to very quickly say silently what you want, or who you want to be, or what you want to do. I just made a wish. I wished that Wuyu would call me Papa one day. Will you remember to make a wish the next time you see a shooting star?"

I stayed with her for a long time. The sky was still indigo, dotted by a few twinkling stars. At some point I went into my study for a smoke. Collapsing into a chair, I took a long drag and exhaled, a simple action that loosened me up like a dry tealeaf uncurling in water. Wuyu pushed the half-opened door and stuck her head in to look at me before running off. I called out to her as I got up and walked into the living room. She was standing at the window again, looking out, just like before. When I drew closer, she turned to look at me, as if to make sure I was there behind her. I bent down to look up from her angle; the sky was the same indigo, with the same few stars. But there had to be more—the view outside would not have been enough to make her go find me.

"Tell Papa, Wuyu, why do you want Papa here?" I knew she wouldn't answer, but I paused and went on anyway. "Did you see something?" She turned and looked at me, but quickly looked away. "Did you see a kitty? Or a puppy?"

I could not figure out what possibly could have appeared at this hour outside the window for her to see. What was it she wanted me to look at? In the windowpane I saw the reflection of her face tilted up at the sky; I was touched by the lovely yet sad expression. When I gently moved up to put my arms around her from behind, she leaned back against me with her eyes still fixed on the sky. Can anyone know a father's happiness at such a moment? Yet whenever we felt happy because of her, that was also the moment of our greatest pain. There was nothing we could do, though, except to wordlessly beseech the blue sky, as the saying goes. That was why we had nicknamed her Wuyu, wordless.

It took a long time before she finally dozed off. *Shh—don't wake her up.* I had stayed in the same position since I'd put my arms around her, and now my body and my arms were numb and sore. I wasn't sure I could carry her to bed without waking her up. My wife came out just then and gently took her from me, giving me the opportunity to slowly stretch and loosen up, like a python waking up from hibernation. I was still working on my tight muscles when she came back from tucking in our daughter.

"Were you awake?" It was an innocuous question, but it drew a pointed response.

"How could I sleep?" Ignoring her, I struggled to raise my stiff arms. "Do you remember how you used to fall asleep with your head on my arm when we were dating? It was sore and numb, but I didn't dare move it, and by the time you woke up, it was dead."

"You're in a joking mood tonight, I see." She laughed, too.

"That was true. It wasn't a joke." She enjoyed red wine, so I suggested, "Is that half-bottle of red wine still good? It was opened quite a while ago. Let's finish it off tonight."

While she went to get the bottle, I put on a newly purchased CD and let "Time to Say Goodbye" by Andrea Bocelli flow softly in the room. I loved his Latin flair and the way his throaty voice faded at the end, like a fire burning itself out. Wearing a bright smile, my wife returned with two glasses and the bottle.

"Don't get any ideas tonight," she whispered.

"No?"

"No."

Some people's happiness can arouse jealousy. Since we'd had Wuyu, whenever we enjoyed a moment of happiness, like taking a little time for ourselves, there was always something that would warn us not to get complacent. No sooner had we softly touched our glasses than we heard the sound of her labored breathing as she struggled for air. Startled, we ran to her room; she was curled up, writhing and gasping, her face turning purple. We rushed her to the ER while calling for her regular physician, Dr. Cai, who tried to comfort us when he noticed the guilty look on our faces—we did live out in a suburb, but there was no untimely delay on anyone's part. No one could have foreseen such an urgent case me Papa one day? Did you? Did you make that wish? Or did you wish to become a canary? Yes, of course. You wished you could be a singing canary. Papa knows that."

We walked along when her body was taken to the morgue. When the worker there was about to slide the drawer in, my wife fell apart and grabbed the side of it, refusing to let him push Wuyu in. She howled as I tried to pry her fingers off. I was surprised to find that her hands were harder and colder than the steel, and they shocked me out of my dazed state. A searing pain tore through my heart as I looked at everything in the morgue. I knew that I was teetering on the point of a total breakdown. With great effort and some lies, I managed to cajole my wife into leaving with me, but she resisted along the way, madly pounding my head at every step until we were out of the morgue. She collapsed when the door closed behind us. The worker came out and helped me take her to the emergency room. The doctor took one look at me and said that I, too, was in need of an IV. So my wife and I ended up lying in separate beds in the hallway as we waited for her to recover.

I did not agree with my wife that grief was making me incoherent, for I was convinced that Wuyu had seen a shooting star and had made a wish at the window. Her wish, I assumed, was to become a canary. That was the only possibility, and I would be crazy to believe that it could be anything else. How would I not know, since I had raised her? When spring thunder brought rain earlier in the year, canaries started to sing, and I took one home with me. Wuyu, who had never been attached to anything, had been steadfast and devoted, insisting on feeding the bird and changing the water herself. Though clumsy at first, she was willing to learn and actually did the work when we asked her to wipe up spilled water with a rag or clean up with a broom. She spent more time caring for the bird than doing anything else. Which was why I believed that she had seen a shooting star and made a wish to become a canary. Happy with my conclusion, I turned to look at my wife, eager to share my idea, but she was sleeping, the effect of a tranquilizer in the drips. A nurse told me she'd be awake in an hour.

It was getting light outside. On our way home, I had a serious talk with my wife about two things. First, I told her that Wuyu had seen a shooting star; otherwise she would not have come to me in the study. And our daughter did wish to be a canary. My wife's eyes snapped open to glare at me when she heard the last phrase. I could understand why she refused to believe me; she had been in our bedroom at the time. I did not want to argue. Second, I suggested to her that we not tell anyone about Wuyu's death. That got her attention, and she turned to look at me. "Hear me out first. These have been exhausting years, and I don't know how long it will take us to recover from this devastating blow. If we tell people about it, can you imagine how many friends and family members will come to see us? Sure, they'll come with condolences, but we will still have to answer the same questions over and over. When you repeat the same answer too many times, your expression no longer matches the severity of the event, and that would be weird. This is not something we can get over in a day or two."

"Not even my parents?"

"I'm not telling my mother yet, and I don't care what they say later. We'll suffer a breakdown if we don't rest and give ourselves some peace. Your nerves have been stretched too thin for too long, don't you think?"

My contradiction scared me. I was convinced that Wuyu had

turned into a canary, but I could deal with it calmly and rationally. My wife turned her head and closed her eyes, which I took as a sign of consent.

The canary started singing when I was looking for the house keys outside our door. I froze.

"Open the door, will you?"

"Did you hear the canary singing?"

"Please don't talk about the canary anymore, all right?"

I could see how the bird had become a reminder of grief for my wife. But it was different for me, because I believed that my daughter had made a wish to be a canary. The fact was there, and I wasn't going against the principle of knowable truth. I even hoped I'd see two birds when I walked in, telling myself that I hadn't lost my mind, as my wife claimed.

She went straight to our bedroom the moment I opened the door, leaving me in the living room to hear the bird sing, its crisp melody creating a brief illusion that there were two of them. But this was strange. How had the cloth fallen to the floor? Had Wuyu done that? Not unlikely. In addition to the fallen cloth, the bird was singing in a louder voice this morning. Eager to share my discovery, I headed over to the bedroom, but stopped when I recalled her frosty request: "Please don't talk about the canary anymore, all right?" I turned to look at the bird, which was acting differently; it was jumping around more than usual, and making shrill, agitated sounds. It turned to look at me, ignoring the bamboo perches, when I put my face up to the cage. It looked just like Wuyu. Yes, it was our daughter's face. What to do now? Lowering my voice so my wife wouldn't hear me, I called out softly, "Wuyu, Wuyu. Wuyu—"

Anything can be overcome, no matter how difficult, as long as there is life. I often expressed concern that even after a lot of time had passed, she still could not bring herself to go into Wuyu's room. Not that she stayed away altogether, but the few times she did go in, she cried so hard she couldn't move, and it took some effort for me to get her out. She retaliated by saying I was losing my mind grieving over our daughter whenever she thought I was spending too much time playing with the bird.

One day there was a TV news special on shooting stars in the constellation Leo that got me thinking. I suggested to my wife that we go watch shooting stars on the mountain one night. I knew I had violated a taboo the moment the words were out. Shooting stars, canaries, and Wuyu had formed a series of loaded signs between us. Several times she had told me in no uncertain terms to stop with the nonsense about our daughter turning into a canary. This time, however, when the reference slipped out, her only reaction was to say offhandedly that I should go by myself, that she wasn't interested. I didn't want to ask again, in case it was a sad reminder and she would say something that would keep me from going. I put a portable stereo system in the car, along with the Bocelli CD, before driving up to the mountain.

It was nearly eleven when I got there. The spot had been a trysting spot for my wife and me eight years before. Based on her calculation, it was where Wuyu had been conceived. The acacia grove was denser than before, but the grassy area behind it remained unchanged, with short couch grass surrounding a rocky ridge. Sweeping the dry leaves off the rock surface with my feet, I cleared enough space to lie down. It was quiet all around, so quiet it made me flinch. When the music began to play, however, it turned into a different place, and I was able to relax. I gazed into the sky when everything was ready, then lay down to look up.

"Will anyone show up?" I heard my wife ask. "Who would come to a place like this?"

I marveled at the shooting stars arcing across the eastern sky. The grass towered over me as I lay there, but it didn't swallow me up; I simply shrank. I was so insubstantial that my heart turned frail and brittle. A stream of hot tears coursed down over both of my temples, and the starry sky blurred in my vision; the overlapping sights before me were spectacular, dazzling my eyes when I looked in the direction of the shooting stars.

My future wife was crying; we weren't married yet.

"Are you sad?"

She shook her head.

"Are you afraid?"

She gave me an unhappy look. Later, after we were married, she told me how wide of the mark my wild guesses had been. It was the contented reaction of a woman deeply touched by happiness, she said.

The cool breeze slowly dried the tears in my eyes, and I was able to see shooting stars pouring down like rain. Afraid I would miss my chance, I quickly made a crazy mixture of wishes related to Wuyu.

When I got home the following morning, I realized that I had turned into a birdcage for Wuyu, who was leaping merrily inside me, the rhythmic movements causing me to sway cheerfully from side to side. The hourly news was looping in the living room; the TV had obviously been on all night. The screen showed the aftermath of a car accident on a twisting mountain highway; the car being hoisted up from the ravine was mine. No wonder my wife was slumped on the sofa in front of the TV, looking as if she had just regained consciousness. She was staring into space, muttering to herself, "How am I going to go on?" She seemed incapable of saying anything else. I said to Wuyu, "Mama is silly. You and I are still here."

After staying up all night, I was so exhausted that all I wanted to do was sleep. A pillow was pressed down on my face, waking me up from my deep, sweet slumber. I struggled to get up, but my wife wouldn't give up, and kept hitting me with the pillow.

"How could you make me a widow?" She laughed. "You're awful, horrible."

"What do you mean, make you a widow?" I was confused.

"What's this?" She brought a manuscript out from behind her back. "What do you have to say for yourself?"

"Oh, that." I laughed. "Use your head. It's a story written in the first person. The I is a fictional character, not me. This is precisely the reason why I never wrote a first-person love story."

"I know, I know. Why must you always think I know nothing?"

"But it still feels kind of weird, doesn't it?"

"No." She laughed again.

"You wouldn't admit it if it did," I said, and got a few more hits with the pillow.

"Still working on it?"

"I worked till early this morning and was too tired to finish it. What do you think?"

"Not bad."

"What if it weren't by your husband?"

"I do know, of course, and it's better than not bad."

"I think there are still some problems."

"Wait here." She walked out. Shortly I heard her surprised shout in the living room.

"Ah! Wuyu! You, you're back?!"

"Mama." It was the sound of a long-suffering girl.

"What? Are you calling me Mama, Wuyu? You're really calling me Mama. Come here, come call your father Papa and make him happy." My wife sounded shrill from the excitement.

My hair stood on end, and I sat up in fright. My wife's face appeared in the doorway, looking to the side at Wuyu, who was behind her. *My wife is still the top-rated theater actress she was all those years ago,* I said to myself. She shifted her gaze to look at me as Wuyu ran up.

2002

Dragon-Eye Well

In a remote village there was a deep well shared by everyone. In olden times a geomancer had said it was the eye of a dragon, so that became the name of the well and the name of the village. Naturally, everyone who lived there, adults and children alike, was called a Dragon-Eye Well villager.

Usually the well was like the sun on clear days, and sometimes it was the spot where children could be closest to the moon and the stars. In the middle of the day, the sun slowly and inched toward the well, into which it slipped for a cool bath to make itself sparkle like gold. Then it climbed out and returned to the sky.

The village children all had to help out by drawing water from the well for their families. The young boys and girls honed their water-drawing skills to perfection. You should have seen how they wound the long bucket rope around one hand before lowering it down to just above the surface. When all movement was stilled, they jerked the rope to make the bucket do a half-somersault, then let it slip so the bucket could drink its fill as it was swallowed up by the well water. It was then time to bring up the full bucket. Younger children who tagged along watched with envy, and no of cardiovascular complications, even if she had been staying in the hospital. He had, in fact, warned us about such a possibility several years before. We hadn't believed him at first and had even taken Wuyu to see specialists at Taipei hospitals without telling him, but they'd all said the same thing. That was why our nerves were strained whenever Wuyu showed any unusual signs. Dr. Cai repeatedly stressed that her time was long overdue.

It was strange, however, how I felt I had shed a great burden once Wuyu was gone, even though we were both racked by grief. I was prepared to be pilloried by my wife, who was sobbing in my arms, when I told her how I felt. She looked up at me with tears in her eyes and said in a muffled voice, "Don't let anyone else hear you say that." Her understanding was comforting. Still choking with sadness, I told her how Wuyu had looked into the sky shortly before her fatal episode.

"I'll bet she saw a shooting star and made a wish." I paused. "She must have made a wish. What do you think it could have been?"

I must have sounded foolishly insistent, for she held my head and said, "You're going crazy missing her."

I struggled out of her hands and said, "What kind of wish would she have made? What did she want to do most? What did she like most? What would a sweet seven-year-old girl have wished for?"

I started to cry, fully aware that something out of my control was making me spout nonsense at this moment of extreme grief. Now I understood why, after Father's death, Mother had sobbed in front of his picture, mumbling what sounded to others like gibberish all night long. I felt as if I'd turned into a spectator as I listened to my own gibberish.

"Did you make a wish, Wuyu? Did you wish to speak and call

outsider could ever learn the skill of flipping the bucket on its side.

Sometimes younger boys sneaked over when the bucket wasn't in use and tried to fish the sun out as it cooled off in the well. No boy who had ever grown up in the village could resist so ambitious an endeavor, which would put them on a par with Kuafu, the mythical pursuer of the sun. That is why, from time to time, a child made clumsy by excitement not only failed to catch the sun, but lost the bucket down the well. When the child fetched a grownup to help, he would suffer a tongue-lashing as the adult fished the bucket and rope out with a wire hook on the end of a bamboo laundry pole. Every boy lied about trying to catch the sun when asked why he was fooling around at the well, though the adults knew the truth, because they had grown up the same way. But they did not let on, out of a fear of losing their authority, especially those who were now fathers and grandfathers.

On clear nights, stars also came for the well water, though they usually had a bit of fun before remembering to take the water back into the sky. On days around the first and the fifteenth of each lunar month, when Lady Moon passed by the well, she stopped to study her face and fix her makeup.

When the people of Taiwan no longer ate so much rice, the children of Dragon-Eye Well Village grew up and left for urban areas. Those who remained grew old and lacked the strength to draw water from the well. Luckily for them, tap water became available. The aging eye of the dragon faded and went blind.

Ever since then, Grandpa Sun, Moon Lady, and the little stars have stopped coming down. They have stayed in the sky for all time, far, far away from the children down below.

2005

www.ingramcontent.com/pod-product-compliance
Lightning Source LLC
Chambersburg PA
CBHW021023110526
R18276100001B/R182761PG44588CBX00015B/27